Competing with Flexible Lateral Organizations

Second Edition

Competing with Flexible Lateral Organizations

Second Edition

Jay R. Galbraith
Center for Effective Organizations
University of Southern California

ADDISON-WESLEY PUBLISHING COMPANY
Reading, Massachusetts • Menlo Park, California • New York
Don Mills, Ontario • Wokingham, England • Amsterdam • Bonn
Sydney • Singapore • Tokyo • Madrid • San Juan • Milan • Paris

Library of Congress Cataloging-in-Publication Data

Galbraith, Jay R.
    Competing with flexible lateral organizations / Jay R. Galbraith
        p.   cm. — (Addison-Wesley OD series)
    ISBN (invalid) 020150836
    1. Organizational design   2. Decentralization in management.
3. Global organization.   4. Matrix organization.   I. Title.
II. Series: Addison-Wesley series on organization development.
HF58.8.G34   1993
658.4'02—dc20

          93-9857
             CIP

This book is in the Addison-Wesley Series on Organization Development.
Editors: Edgar H. Schein, Richard Beckhard

ISBN 0-201-50836-2
    7 8 9 10-BA-979695·

Other Titles in the Organization Development Series

The Dynamics of Organizational Levels: A Change Framework for Managers and Consultants
Nicholas S. Rashford and David Coghlan

1994 (54323)

This book introduces the idea that, for successful change to occur, organizational interventions have to be coordinated across the major levels of issues that all organizations face. Individual level, team level, inter-unit level, and organizational level issues are identified and analyzed, and the kinds of intervention appropriate to each level are spelled out.

Organization Development: A Process of Learning and Changing, Second Edition
W. Warner Burke

1994 (50835)

This text presents an overview of OD and looks at OD in part as a change of an organization's culture. It looks at the organization and factors that will influence structure and development in the future. The author also introduces new topics such as information management and strategy implementation.

Total Quality: A User's Guide for Implementation
Dan Ciampa

1992 (54992)

This is a book that directly addresses the challenge of how to make Total Quality work in a practical, no-nonsense way. The companies that will dominate markets in the future will be those that deliver high quality, competitively priced products and service just when the customer wants them and in a way that exceeds the customer's expectations. The vehicle by which these companies move to that stage is Total Quality.

Parallel Learning Structures: Increasing Innovation in Bureaucracies
Gervase R. Bushe and A.B. Shani

1991 (52427)

Parallel learning structures are technostructural interventions that promote system-wide change in bureaucracies while retaining the advantages of bureaucratic design. This text serves as a resource of models and theories built around five cases of parallel learning structures that can help those who create and maintain them be more effective and successful. For those new to parallel learning structures, the text provides practical advice as to when and how to use them.

Managing in the New Team Environment: Skills, Tools, and Methods

Larry Hirschhorn

1991 (52503)

This text is designed to help manage the tensions and complexities that arise for managers seeking to guide employees in a team environment. Based on an interactive video course developed at IBM, the text takes managers step by step through the process of building a team and authorizing it to act while they learn to step back and delegate. Specific issues addressed are how to give a team structure, how to facilitate its basic processes, and how to acknowledge differences in relationships among team members and between the manager and individual team members.

Leading Business Teams: How Teams Can Use Technology and Group Process Tools to Enhance Performance

Robert Johansen, David Sibbett, Suzyn Benson, Alexia Martin, Robert Mittman, and Paul Saffo

1991 (52829)

What technology or tools should organization development people or team leaders have at their command, now and in the future? This text explores the intersection of technology and business teams, a new and largely uncharted area that goes by several labels, including "groupware," a term that encompasses both electronic and nonelectronic tools for teams. This is the first book of its kind from the field describing what works for business teams and what does not.

The Conflict-Positive Organization: Stimulate Diversity and Create Unity

Dean Tjosvold

1991 (51485)

This book describes how managers and employees can use conflict to find common ground, solve problems, and strengthen morale and relationships. By showing how well-managed conflict invigorates and empowers teams and organizations, the text demonstrates how conflict is vital for a company's continuous improvement and increased competitive advantage.

Change by Design
Robert R. Blake, Jane Srygley Mouton, and Anne Adams McCanse

1989 (50748)

This book develops a systematic approach to organization development and provides readers with rich illustrations of coherent planned change. The book involves testing, examining, revising, and strengthening conceptual foundations in order to create sharper corporate focus and increased predictability of successful organization development.

Organization Development in Health Care
R. Wayne Boss

1989 (18364)

This is the first book to discuss the intricacies of the health care industry. The book explains the impact of OD in creating healthy and viable organizations in the health care sector. Through unique and innovative techniques, hospitals are able to reduce nursing turnover, thereby resolving the nursing shortage problem. The text also addresses how OD can improve such bottom-line variables as cash flow and net profits.

Self-Designing Organizations: Learning How to Create High Performance
Susan Albers Mohrman and Thomas G. Cummings

1989 (14603)

This book looks beyond traditional approaches to organizational transition, offering a strategy for developing organizations that enables them to learn not only how to adjust to the dynamic environment in which they exist, but also how to achieve a higher level of performance. This strategy assumes that change is a learning process: the goal is continually refined as organizational members learn how to function more effectively and respond to dynamic conditions in their environment.

Power and Organization Development: Mobilizing Power to Implement Change
Larry E. Greiner and Virginia E. Schein

1988 (12185)

This book forges an important collaborative approach between two opposing and often contradictory approaches to management: OD practitioners who espouse a "more humane" workplace without understanding the political realities of getting things done, and practicing managers who feel comfortable with power but overlook the role of human potential in contributing to positive results.

Designing Organizations for High Performance
David P. Hanna

1988 (12693)

This book is the first to give insight into the actual processes you can use to translate organizational concepts into bottom-line improvements. Hanna's "how-to" approach shows not only the successful methods of intervention, but also the plans behind them and the corresponding results.

Process Consultation, Volume 1: Its Role in Organization Development, Second Edition
Edgar H. Schein

1988 (06736)

How can a situation be influenced in the workplace without the direct use of power or formal authority? This book presents the core theoretical foundations and basic prescriptions for effective management.

Organizational Transitions: Managing Complex Change, Second Edition
Richard Beckhard and Reuben T. Harris

1987 (10887)

This book discusses the choices involved in developing a management system appropriate to the "transition state." It also discusses commitment to change, organizational culture, and increasing and maintaining productivity, creativity, and innovation.

Organization Development: A Normative View
W. Warner Burke

1987 (10697)

This book concisely describes and defines the theories and practices of organization development and also looks at organization development as change in an organization's culture. It is a useful guide to the field of organization development and is invaluable to managers, executives, practitioners, and anyone desiring an excellent overview of this multifaceted field.

Team Building: Issues and Alternatives, Second Edition
William G. Dyer

1987 (18037)

Through the use of the techniques and procedures described in this book, managers and consultants can effectively prepare, apply, and follow up on the human processes affecting the productive functioning of teams.

The Technology Connection: Strategy and Change in the Information Age

Marc S. Gerstein

1987 (12188)

This is a book that guides managers and consultants through crucial decisions about the use of technology for increasing effectiveness and competitive advantage. It provides a useful way to think about the relationship between information technology, business strategy, and the process of change in organizations.

Stream Analysis: A Powerful Way to Diagnose and Manage Organizational Change

Jerry I. Porras

1987 (05693)

Drawing on a conceptual framework that helps the reader to better understand organizations, this book shows how to diagnose failings in organizational functioning and how to plan a comprehensive set of actions needed to change the organization into a more effective system.

Process Consultation, Volume II: Lessons for Managers and Consultants

Edgar H. Schein

1987 (06744)

This book shows the viability of the process consultation model for working with human systems. Like Schein's first volume on process consultation, the second volume focuses on the moment-to-moment behavior of the manager or consultant rather than on the design of the OD program.

Managing Conflict: Interpersonal Dialogue and Third-Party Roles, Second Edition

Richard E. Walton

1987 (08859)

This book shows how to implement a dialogue approach to conflict management. It presents a framework for diagnosing recurring conflicts and suggests several basic options for controlling or resolving them.

Pay and Organization Development

Edward E. Lawler

1981 (03990)

This book examines the important role that reward systems play in organization development efforts. By combining examples and specific recommendations with conceptual material, it organizes the various topics and puts them into a total systems perspective. Specific pay approaches such as gainsharing, skill-based pay, and flexible benefits are discussed and their impact on productivity and the quality of work life is analyzed.

Work Redesign
J. Richard Hackman and Greg R. Oldham
1980 (02779)

This book is a comprehensive, clearly written study of work design as a strategy for personal and organizational change. Linking theory and practical technologies, it develops traditional and alternative approaches to work design that can benefit both individuals and organizations.

Organizational Dynamics: Diagnosis and Intervention
John P. Kotter
1978 (03890)

This book offers managers and OD specialists a powerful method of diagnosing organizational problems and of deciding when, where, and how to use (or not use) the diverse and growing number of organizational improvement tools that are available today. Comprehensive and fully integrated, the book includes many different concepts, research findings, and competing philosophies and provides specific examples of how to use the information to improve organizational functioning.

Career Dynamics: Matching Individual and Organizational Needs
Edgar H. Schein
1978 (06834)

This book studies the complexities of career development from both an individual and an organizational perspective. Changing needs throughout the adult life cycle, interaction of work and family, and integration of individual and organizational goals through human resource planning and development are all thoroughly explored.

Matrix
Stanley M. Davis and Paul Lawrence
1977 (01115)

This book defines and describes the matrix organization, a significant departure from the traditional "one man-one boss" management system. The author notes that the tension between the need for independence (fostering innovation) and order (fostering efficiency) drives organizations to consider a matrix system. Among the issues addressed are reasons for using a matrix, methods for establishing one, the impact of the system on individuals, its hazards, and what types of organizations can use a matrix system.

Feedback and Organization Development: Using Data-Based Methods

David A. Nadler

1977 (05006)

This book addresses the use of data as a tool for organizational change. It attempts to bring together some of what is known from experience and research and to translate that knowledge into useful insights for those who are thinking about using data-based methods in organizations. The broad approach of the text is to treat a whole range of questions and issues considering the various uses of data as an organizational change tool.

Designing Complex Organizations

Jay Galbraith

1973 (02559)

This book attempts to present an analytical framework of the design of organizations, particularly of types of organizations that apply lateral decision processes or matrix forms. These forms have become pervasive in all types of organizations, yet there is little systematic public knowledge about them. This book helps fill this gap.

Organization Development: Strategies and Models

Richard Beckhard

1969 (00448)

This book is written for managers, specialists, and students of management who are concerned with the planning of organization development programs to resolve the dilemmas brought about by a rapidly changing environment. Practiced teams of interdependent people must spend real time improving their methods of working, decision making, and communicating, and a planned, managed change is the first step toward effecting and maintaining these improvements.

Organization Development: Its Nature, Origins, and Prospects

Warren G. Bennis

1969 (00523)

This primer on OD is written with an eye toward the people in organizations who are interested in learning more about this educational strategy as well as for those practitioners and students of OD who may want a basic statement both to learn from and to argue with. The author treats the subject with a minimum of academic jargon and a maximum of concrete examples drawn from his own and others' experience.

Developing Organizations: Diagnosis and Action

Paul R. Lawrence and Jay W. Lorsch

1969 (04204)

This book is a personal statement of the authors' evolving experience, through research and consulting, in the work of developing organizations. The text presents the authors' overview of organization development, then proceeds to examine issues at each of three critical interfaces: the organization-environment interface, the group-group interface, and the individual-organization interface, including brief examples of work on each. The text concludes by pulling the themes together in a set of conclusions about organizational development issues as they present themselves to practicing managers.

About the Author

Jay R. Galbraith is a Professor of Management and Organization and a Senior Research Scientist at the Center for Effective Organizations at USC. His principal areas of research are in organizational design, change, and development; strategy and organization at the corporate, business unit, and international levels of analysis; and international partnering arrangements including joint ventures and network-type organizations. Dr. Galbraith has had considerable consulting experience in the United States, Europe, Asia, and South America. He has written numerous articles for professional journals, handbooks, and research collections. His most recently published works are *Strategy Implementation: The Role of Structure and Process* (with Rob Kazanjian), West Publishing, and *Organizing for the Future* (with Ed Lawler), Jossey-Bass 1993.

Foreword

The Addison-Wesley Series on Organization Development originated in the late 1960s when a number of us recognized that the rapidly growing field of "OD" was not well understood or well defined. We also recognized that there was no one OD philosophy, and hence one could not at that time write a textbook on the theory and practice of OD, but one could make clear what various practitioners were doing under that label. So the original six books launched what has since become a continuing enterprise, the essence of which was to allow different authors to speak for themselves instead of trying to summarize under one umbrella what was obviously a rapidly growing and highly diverse field.

By the early 1980s the series included nineteen titles. OD was growing by leaps and bounds, and it was expanding into all kinds of organizational areas and technologies of intervention. By this time, many textbooks existed as well that tried to capture core concepts of the field, but we felt that diversity and innovation were still the more salient aspects of OD.

Now as we move into the 1990s our series includes over thirty titles, and we are beginning to see some real convergence in the underlying assumptions of OD. As we observe how different professionals working in different kinds of organizations and occupational communities make their case, we see we are still far from having a single "theory" of organization development. Yet, a set of common assumptions is surfacing. We are beginning to see patterns in what works and what does not work, and we are becoming more articulate about these patterns. We are also seeing the field increasingly connected to other organizational sciences and disciplines such as information technology, coordination theory, and organization theory. In the early 1990s we saw several important themes described with Ciampa's *Total Quality* showing the important link to employee involvement in continuous improvement, Johansen et al.'s *Leading Business Teams* exploring the important arena of electronic information tools for teamwork, Tjosvold's *The Conflict-Positive Organization* showing how conflict management can turn conflict into constructive action, Hirschhorn's *Managing in the New Team Environment* building bridges to group psychodynamic theory, and Bushe and Shani's *Parallel Learning Structures* providing an integrative theory for large-scale organization change.

We continue this trend with two revisions and one wholly new approach. Burke has taken his highly successful *Organization Development* into new realms with an updating and expansion. Galbraith has updated and enlarged his classic theory of how information management is at the heart of organization design with his new edition entitled *Competing with Flexible Lateral Organizations,* and Rashford and Coghlan have introduced the important concept of levels of organizational complexity as a basis for intervention theory in their book entitled *The Dynamics of Organizational Levels.*

We welcome these revisions and new titles and will continue to explore the various frontiers of organization development with additional titles as we identify themes that are relevant to the ever more difficult problem of helping organizations to remain effective in an increasingly turbulent environment.

New York, New York   Richard H. Beckhard
Cambridge, Massachusetts   Edgar H. Schein

Preface

This book is the result of several factors coming together at about the same time. The publisher, Addison-Wesley, asked me several times to revise *Designing Complex Organizations,* my first book in this series. Until recently, however, I had neither the energy nor the content to do a revision.

Then, in 1986, I joined Ed Lawler at the Center for Effective Organizations at the University of Southern California. The Center is a great halfway house with an academic Mission to do "useful research." I then recruited my longtime client Gianfranco Gambigliani, from FIAT, to become a sponsor. Gianfranco and FIAT's education subsidiary, ISVOR, have provided me with challenging assignments since the early 1970s. One of his assignments was to have the Center work with him and FIAT management to learn how companies are changing their organizations to remain competitive. From this assignment I began looking at organization as a competitive tool with which to gain advantage.

Part of the FIAT project involved conducting visits with teams of FIAT managers to leading-edge companies to study how they were using their organizations to compete. Along with partnering, these companies (American, European, and Japanese) were extensively using lateral forms of organization to gain speed, coordinate international subsidiaries, or combine business-unit strengths. They all wanted flexibility in responding quickly to rapidly changing situations. I felt quite at home during these discussions. The most popular parts of *Designing Complex Organizations* were the chapters on lateral relations and matrix organization. Since its publication, I have spent a great deal of time with companies implementing product management, project management, and matrix organizations. Here, with this book, was a chance to update those chapters based on the FIAT project and the notion of competitive advantage.

I felt that there was a need for conceptual clarification. The popular press was portraying teams as a universal solution to all management problems. I had learned that there were costs to using teams. So I have tried in this book to describe the different types and amounts of lateral organization, where the use of teams is one type. I have tried to give guidelines on how to match different types and amounts of lateral organization with different strategies. By using the guidelines, managers can choose the types of teams and team leaders that are appropriate for them.

I also noticed that most discussion of teams was focused on cross-functional teams. Lateral organization is needed here, but I have also encountered it when working across subsidiaries internationally and across business units within the corporation. I have tried to give guidelines for using lateral forms of coordination in all three areas.

One of the things that I have noticed in my experience with many matrix organizations is the great disparity in their effectiveness. Most have been failures. But there are successes. The difference between successful companies and the others is the building of an organizational capability to coordinate across units. Almost always the building of the capability meant developing people who could work in teams, exert influence without authority, and feel comfortable in a variety of settings. These companies built information systems and used planning processes to resolve conflicts. Thus much of the discussion in this book is aimed at management's role in building capability.

Hence the purpose of the book is threefold. First, it is to present lateral organization as a means to gain flexibility and thus competitive advantages in an uncertain world. Second, it is to present guidelines for choosing the types and amounts of lateral organization for implementing different strategies. And third, it is to encourage management to build organizational capability so that lateral organization can be employed when it is needed. I felt that these points would provide useful content based on the Center's useful research.

The energy for this finally came from my wife, Sasha. She said, "When are you going to stop talking and start writing about your experiences?" She convinced me to stop traveling and start writing. Addison-Wesley provided the deadline to complete the package. My thanks to Gianfranco Gambigliani for providing me with the content inspiration for the book. I hope he continues to find my work useful. Thanks also to Sasha. Her help in supporting me as a sounding board, proofreader, and graphic artist makes her a real and valuable partner. But I cannot thank her enough for getting me to take the time to write in the first place.

Breckenridge, Colorado   J. R. G.

Contents

1

Lateral Organizational Capability

This book is about building organizational capability. It is about building a specific kind of organizational capability—the lateral organization. The concept of organizational capability is not a new one. It has been implied in analyses using strengths and weaknesses. It has been implied in the listing of pros and cons for choosing either a functional or a product organizational structure. But the identification of organization as a capability to be built and sustained is new. And the use of an organizational capability as a competitive tool is also new. This book provides an argument for using organizational capability in general—and lateral organizational capability in particular—as a competitive advantage. The main focus, however, will be on how to create, design, and build the various types of lateral organizational capability.

The next section of this chapter attempts to state briefly the case for organizational capability; there are some good reasons why organizational capability has become a priority. Then the concept of organizational capability is defined. Next, the subject of lateral organization is defined and described. Along with lateral organization, the vertical, hierarchical organization requires some discussion. Though it is popular to speak of non-hierarchical organizations, the vertical structure is still fundamental, though there is room for much modification. The author's positions on these issues are presented before moving to lateral coordination and lateral organization.

The Importance of Organizational Capability

In the 1980s, theorists from a number of points of view all came to regard capabilities and competencies as an important and sustainable source of competitive advantage. Central to the convergence was the belief that traditional sources of competitive advantage do not last very long. Economies of scale and barriers to entry are circumvented with various types of partnerships. Unique products and technologies are easily and quickly copied. Therefore, unique internal management processes and intangible resources, which are less visible and less easily copied, have come to be seen as potential sustainable sources of advantage. Economists and strategic management theorists now describe internal resource-based advantages and even a resource-based theory of the firm (Wernerfelt, 1984; Grant, 1991). Other strategists see companies competing based on their core competence (Hamel and Prahalad, 1990) and capabilities (Stalk, Evans, and Shulman, 1992).

Another factor enhancing the priority of organizational capability is the increasing investment in intangible assets. Between 1977 and 1990, such countries as Japan, Germany, and the United States increased their investments in R&D from 1 percent of GNP to 3 percent. If we add to that the increases in investments in education, training, management development, management processes, and software, it is clear that competition in developed countries centers around investing in intangible or invisible assets (Itami, 1987), which result in knowledge products, or products of the brain. Indeed, some say that from now on competitive advantage will be man-made (Thurow, 1992). If competitive advantage is man-made, then companies will compete on the effectiveness of the human talent they attract and how well it is coordinated in serving the needs of the customer: that is, competition will center around organizational capability. Edward Lawler calls this capability the "ultimate advantage" (Lawler, 1992).

With the heightening level of competition, most firms will experience a greater level of rivalry in their markets. This rivalry gives more choice to the customer. More choice to the customer requires more responsiveness from companies to satisfy that choice. Thus, companies need responsiveness and organizational flexibility in responding to increased customer choice.

Lateral organization is a major source of flexibility in responding to choosy customers.

There is also an increased recognition among managers of the importance of organizational capability. In the past, organization was synonymous with structure. As a result, it was devalued. A common belief among managers was, "People are important. Just give me good people and they will make any organization work." Today, managers are learning that capabilities such as the Toyota Production System (TPS) (Womack, Jones, and Roos, 1990) are not based solely on good people. The TPS is, in fact, an intricate blend of manufacturing techniques, human resource practices, teamwork, and relations with suppliers. It is an organizational capability that many others are struggling to duplicate. Similarly, 3M has created an organization that is capable of creating innovative new products. It is not based solely on good people. Many managers have visited the 3M campus in St. Paul, but very few have duplicated their innovation. There are other examples, but the point is that more and more managers are seeing the organizational capability built by top-performing companies as being key to their success.

In summary, the decline of traditional sources of advantage, the increasing investments in intangible assets, and the heightened levels of rivalry in markets have all combined to focus the attention of leading theorists on the importance of capabilities in general, and organizational capabilities in particular. Increasingly, managers are seeing the value of building capability into their organization. The next section defines what organizational capability is.

What Is Organizational Capability?

A company builds capabilities as it grows and develops. The stages of its evolution can be seen as a sequence of adding capabilities to the company's repertoire (Galbraith, 1982). At each stage, there is a task to be performed and mastered. The organization acquires a capability when it can consistently and effectively execute the task. By that time, the company has figured out what kinds of people perform the task best, what information they need, how to measure performance, and how to structure the effort. Figure 1.1, which will be frequently referred to

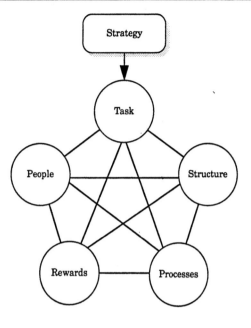

Figure 1.1
Star Model

throughout the text as the Star Model, shows the elements that must be created and combined in an organization to support task performance, and thereby create the organizational capability (Galbraith, 1987).

The Star Model conveys the message that the business strategy determines which tasks are important and require an organizational capability. The company then must put into place organizational structures, management processes, rewards and incentives, and the people or human resource practices that support the task performance. An organizational capability is created when all of the organizational elements on the Star Model are *aligned* and *support* task performance.

The following will serve as an example of the Star Model: A company competes on the basis of frequent and rapid introduction of new products or services. To build a new product development capability, it would create a structure of new product departments in each of the key functional areas. The structure minimizes interfaces and facilitates communication across functions. Each department would dedicate a member to a team for each product being introduced. Management would create a new product information system to support the product development decision process. A management council would set priorities and move resources so all product programs stay on track. Product team members would all have access to an integrated data base containing all data concerning their new product program. Key team members may be co-located to facilitate face-to-face communication. All key team members would follow careers of cross-functional rotation and have skill-based compensation plans. In this way, all the structures, processes, rewards, and people practices are aligned with each other and with the task of developing new products rapidly and frequently. When fully implemented, the company will have acquired the capability to work across functions to introduce new products.

This new product development capability is a lateral organizational capability, in that different functions are coordinated without communicating through the hierarchy. People in different functions communicate directly with each other, rather than through their respective managers. There are other kinds of organizational capabilities that will not be directly addressed in this book. Corning Glass has developed a capability for creating and managing partnerships. 3M has created a capability to create and grow new businesses. These capabilities and others all require aligning strategies, structures, processes, rewards, and people practices in a supportive manner, as indicated in the star model.

It is the different kinds of lateral capabilities that will be discussed in this book. There are three basic types of lateral organization. One, coordination across functions, was described for new products. Another is coordination across business units in a diversified corporation. The third is international coordination of activities across countries and regions. All three types are based on the same set of concepts. However, they present three different implementation problems. A capability created in one area does not guarantee that the company will be effective in another area. Capabilities need to be created separately in each area.

Before describing the different types of lateral organization, some definitions of lateral and vertical organization are necessary.

The Lateral Organization

The lateral organization, no matter what its form, is *a mechanism for decentralizing general management decisions.* It accomplishes the decentralization by recreating the organization in microcosm for the issue at hand. That is, each organization unit with information about—and a stake in—an issue contributes a representative for issue resolution, as shown in Fig. 1.2. This group is the equivalent of a general manager for the issue being addressed. To the extent that this kind of group can convene, problem solve, decide upon an action, and communicate the result and execute it, the organization has created a lateral organization. When the lateral organization is created, consistently and effectively, the company has created a lateral capability.

There are a number of advantages that accrue for the company with a lateral capability. The first is that the lateral organization increases the capacity of the entire organization to make more decisions more often. In a business world of constant change and adaptation, the organization must have the ability to constantly decide and re-decide its activities. The increase in capacity is achieved by decentralizing some decisions, thereby freeing up management time for other decisions. This division of

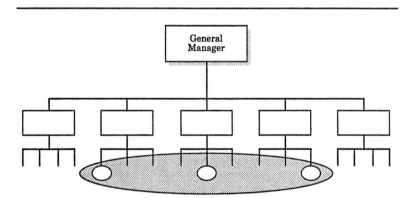

Figure 1.2
Lateral Organization Across the Hierarchy

labor is a second advantage. Management can focus on longer run and more external issues, while people with direct product and customer contact can focus on today's issues. The decentralization provided by the lateral organization utilizes the unique perspectives of both groups.

The lateral organization permits the company not only to make more decisions, but also to make different types of decisions. Organizations face many different issues emanating from different suppliers, competitors, partners, products/services, countries, and market segments. The lateral organization allows the resources of the entire organization to be marshaled to focus on these various dimensions. It gives the company the ability to organize around an issue, any issue. Lateral organization creates an ability to be multidimensional and flexible. For example, consulting firms generally use a geographic office structure to focus on clients. But they all have lateral relationships across offices for connecting industry experts and skill (information technology) specialists. The consulting firm can focus, at the least, on the three dimensions of clients, industries, and specialties. Thus the lateral organization can bring a general management, cross-unit perspective to bear on a variety of dimensions.

The lateral organization can lead to better, faster decisions. By decentralizing choice to groups at the point of product and customer contact, decisions can be made and implemented quickly. These groups have access to current and local information. They can act on current information available only to them. By combining decision making and implementation in the same roles, the motivation of the implementers is increased. Thus, cross-unit groups can act quickly, can have access to current information, and can act with high levels of motivation.

Some costs accompany the advantages. First, the decentralized decisions may be no better than those of management. The decisions may be made by less experienced people. They may have current, local information, but may lack the overview to use it in a manner consistent with a general manager's perspective. These costs are simply those of any delegated decision. There has always been a trade-off between fast, parochial, delegated decisions and slower, global decisions. Of course, local, parochial perspectives can be reduced by providing global information, teaching people about the business and business strategy, and giving them a global incentive. Thus, part of the task of organization design is to reduce the classical negatives in any trade-off design choice.

Another cost is the time of the people involved in communicating and deciding on cross-unit issues. Time that people spend communicating with others in other units is time not spent with customers or suppliers or developing new members. The lateral organization is an investment in management time to address issues such as new product development. The strategy places priorities on those issues that require the investments.

A third cost is the increased level of conflict. Each member of a different unit will see the issue differently and have different preferences. Much of the deciding and communicating in the lateral organization is devoted to resolving conflicts. Of course, the more skilled the organization's members are in conflict resolution, the lower the cost and the less time and energy invested in reaching a decision.

In summary, the lateral organization is the decentralization of general management issues to be resolved by working across organizational units. The lateral capability is created when all the elements in the Star Model have been created and aligned. There are three general types of lateral organizations: One type coordinates across functions, the second type coordinates across business units, and the third type coordinates across countries. The ability to coordinate laterally increases the number and types of decisions an organization can make. This advantage is created by investing in management time to communicate and decide with people in other organizational units. This lateral organization works across the vertical organization structure. The next section discusses the vertical organization.

Lateral and Vertical Organization

The implementation of a lateral organization assumes that a vertical and hierarchical organization already exists. The lateral organization then coordinates work that takes place in a number of different organizational units within this vertical organization. As we will see, it is easier and faster to use the lateral organization for many tasks. However, there has been a lot of discussion recently about eliminating the hierarchy. Some suggest that we should have nonhierarchical organizational structures. The author's position is that this view is partly correct and partly exaggerated.

The nonhierarchical position is correct in the sense that organizational structures are becoming less hierarchical. The efforts that companies are making, however, are really attempts to eliminate the dysfunctional effects of hierarchy. Hierarchies of status and rank create barriers to communication across ranks and generate managerial behaviors based on a command and control model. Many companies are currently trying to remove status and rank differences, which imply higher and lower classes of employees. For example, all workers are becoming salaried, time clocks are disappearing for some (or clocks introduced for all), first-come/first-served parking lots are being used, and executive dining rooms are disappearing. Company structures are becoming flatter as the number of levels is reduced. These changes are likely to continue. All such changes are intended to remove barriers to communication, eliminate animosity between ranks, and make the decision process faster and more efficient (Lawler, 1988).

In another sense, the predictions of the death of hierarchy are greatly exaggerated. Hierarchy arises because of the complexities of the information-processing requirements of the large-scale organization (Galbraith, 1977). We do not have the information and social technologies to allow 1000 people to interact, communicate, and decide upon their collective actions in short time frames; there are simply too many interfaces among 1000 people. The communication complexity is reduced if one person is selected to represent each group of, say, 10 people. This selection process creates a second level of 100 people. While simpler, 100 people is still too many to make the decisions to guide the organization. The second level can also choose a representative for each 10 people and create a third level of 10. This third-level group may then be able to communicate and decide on collective action among themselves. Most organizations further select a leader, a senior partner, a managing director, or a president to act as head of the entire group. But we now have a hierarchical decision process that involves three or four levels of hierarchy. It is the communication and decision processes that require hierarchy to simplify the process of achieving collective action when large numbers of people are interdependent. If these

1000 people were less interdependent, then less coordination would be needed. If these people worked in an investment bank, as opposed to designing and manufacturing a satellite, they would need less communication. Investment bankers could create independent teams of specialists who work on a client's financial issues. Communication within a team is intense. However, communication between teams working for different clients is small. There is a continuous transfer of ideas and decisions to allocate people to teams. But the investment bank's teams can operate relatively autonomously. The teams designing and making a satellite, however, are working on the same project for the same client. They are more interdependent and require more coordination and communication. Conflicts between groups require rapid and continuous resolution. Hierarchy is less, and it is less well-defined in investment banks than in aerospace firms. If more work is going to be done in small autonomous teams, hierarchy will play less of a role in coordination (Peters, 1992). But hierarchy will survive on large, complex projects. So for some time to come, it is likely that organizations will employ a hierarchical decision process.

There are a number of changes, however, that may eventually permit the emergence of nonhierarchical organizations. The first was just discussed: Companies will continue to eliminate the dysfunctional consequences of a hierarchical division of labor. They will continue to eliminate differentials in status, rank, salaries, and perquisites, which create higher and lower classes of employees. Second, the average size of organizations (measured in number of employees) will grow smaller. In part, the decrease will be due to increasing numbers of small and medium-sized enterprises. But also, very large companies, such as General Electric and AT&T, are growing larger in sales volume but smaller in the number of employees. The decrease in the number of employees results from the continuing automation of the work of the first level of employees, the substitution of information technology for white-collar and middle-management level workers, and contracting out for noncore activities. If there are fewer people at the bottom of the hierarchy, there are fewer levels at the top and the average size of organizations and organizational units will continually shrink. Smaller numbers of people translates into fewer levels of hierarchy.

Hierarchy will also decrease with the increasing effectiveness of problem-solving technologies. There is impressive new software which permits large groups of people to communicate and solve problems (Kirkpatrick, 1992). This software has been called Groupware (Johansen, 1988). If groups of 25 to 50 people can communicate and reach consensus on a problem solution in reasonable time frames, larger groups can serve as the first-level building block rather than the 10-person group portrayed above. Groups of 25 to 50 rather than 10 in a 1000-person organization would create a two- to three-level hierarchy rather than a three- to four-level one. So, larger work groups will decrease hierarchy. By increasing the size of the building-block group, putting more activities into the group, and increasing the decision-making power of the group, the need for communication and coordination across groups is decreased. The need for hierarchical communication and decision processes is likewise reduced. However, for organizations with more than a few hundred people scattered around the world, hierarchy will be with us for some time to come.

This chapter focused on definitions of organizational capability in general and lateral organization in particular. The capability to work and coordinate across organizational units creates significant advantages for a company. The next chapter describes the kinds of opportunities to which lateral organization can be applied. Chapter 3 describes the different kinds of lateral forms. The last part of Chapter 3, along with Chapters 4 and 5, present the details of designing the different types of lateral forms for the three types of lateral organization. Chapter 6 is devoted to a particular kind of lateral organization, the distributed organization; a case is used to develop the concept. Chapter 7 presents two summary cases to review the various issues of designing a lateral organizational capability. Chapter 8 presents some summary thoughts.

2

Lateral Coordination

The lateral organization is a mechanism to coordinate activities where portions of a task are carried out in different organizational units. There are numerous occasions when this circumstance arises in today's organizations.

Companies must be capable of coordinating many different kinds of activities. They must be multidimensional and flexible. This chapter describes three kinds of lateral coordination. The first kind is the cross-functional coordination that takes place within a business unit. This type has become widely known because of the Total Quality and Time Compression initiatives. The second kind is coordination across businesses in a diversified corporation. And the third kind is international coordination of business units. As companies locate activities around the world, cross-country coordination is a necessary capability. The diversified company will probably require all three kinds of lateral coordination.

Lateral Coordination—
Multidimensional Coordination

The lateral organization arises to perform the task of lateral coordination; that is, no matter what hierarchical structure is chosen, there are some activities that require coordination across the ranks, rather than up or down the hierarchy. It was said in Chapter 1 that to the extent that we can create larger work groups, place more activities within a group, and delegate decision-making to the group, we will eliminate the need to coordinate across groups. In reality, the creation of such completely self-contained groups almost never happens. The reason is that most organizations deal with a complex, multidimensional world. They have to do business with multiple customers, multiple partners, and multiple suppliers, and compete against multiple rivals in multiple areas of the world. They will deal with multiple governments, regulators, distributors, labor unions, and trade associations. They will employ multiple skill specialties, using multiple technologies while producing multiple products and services. If a company creates an organization to maximize its effectiveness in dealing with one constituency, like customers, it fragments its ability to deal with others. These other dimensions are what require lateral coordination. In this way, concentration on one dimension of the environment inevitably fragments an organization's ability to deal with other dimensions of the environment.

The role of strategy is to prioritize the various dimensions for the organization designer. A company formulates a business strategy by which it will achieve an advantage in the marketplace (Porter, 1985). This strategy will generate criteria the company can use to choose the dimension of the organization structure. This structure will then coordinate the activities to achieve the planned advantage (Galbraith and Kazanjian, 1986). For example, a company may be product-driven. It believes it can achieve an advantage by offering hard-to-copy product features more rapidly than its rivals can. Such a company would choose a product profit center structure with a unit for each type of product. Such a structure maximizes the company's performance in designing unique products with maximum speed. However, a product structure usually irritates a customer who buys from several profit centers and wants one point of contact and one invoice from the company. The company fragments technologies common to all products, as well as fragmenting its buying power with suppliers common to all profit centers. A labor union may want a common contract with several business-unit profit centers. Thus, an organization structure is inevitably a compromise. But it is a compromise driven by criteria from the business strategy. The structure concentrates the performance on the strategic dimensions, and fragments the less important dimensions. It is these fragmented dimensions that require lateral coordination.

As long as the fragmented dimensions were few and/or less important, they could easily be coordinated through the hierarchy. In the example just given, the corporate structure focused on product-line profit centers for its business units, while the hierarchy above them coordinated the less important dimensions across product lines. However, during the 1970s and '80s, the other dimensions increased in both number and importance. The initial response was to solve different coordination problems at different levels and in different parts of the organization. Figure 2.1 shows a typical structure for a multinational company. Functions were coordinated within a business-unit profit center domestically. Country subsidiaries were coordinated in the international division profit center, and the corporation provided coordination across businesses and countries.

Today, companies are experiencing forces that make the old models inadequate. International revenues are more than 50 percent of the total for many companies, and cannot be managed solely by the international division. R&D expenditures are doubling and tripling and cannot be duplicated in every business unit or subsidiary. Time-to-market requirements are half of those in the old product introduction schedules. The result is that there are more and more important coordination issues in addition to those that are managed by the structure shown in Fig. 2.1. Table 2.1 lists the three general types of lateral coordi-

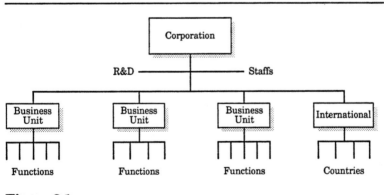

Figure 2.1
Multinational Structure Circa 1980

Table 2.1
Types of Lateral Coordination

1. Cross-Functional Coordination Within a Business Unit
   - Diversity or Variety
   - Unanticipated Changes
   - Work Interdependence
   - Total Quality Initiatives
   - Time Compression

2. Cross-Business-Unit Coordination Within the Corporation
   - Portfolio Diversity
   - Value Added

3. International Coordination Across Country or Geographical Subsidiaries
   - Global Integration
   - Global Dispersion

nation that will be discussed in this book. It is important for the organization designer to understand the variations in these business forces. The different strategies will lead to different amounts of lateral coordination. Different types and amounts of lateral organization will need to be matched with the different amounts of coordination. The remainder of this chapter presents each type, along with the business forces that are making the coordination a priority.

1. Cross-Functional Coordination

The key management challenge for a single business organization is the cross-functional coordination needed to create and deliver products and/or services to customers. This coordination is the task of general managers and their staffs in functional organizations whether they are single-business companies (e.g., Apple Computer) or business units in a multibusiness corporation (e.g., Semiconductors in Motorola). The coordination is most easily accomplished for businesses producing a single product or service that is delivered to a single type of customer. Apple Computer met this condition in the 1980s. It essentially produced a single product, the Macintosh, that went to a single type of customer, computer dealers. The challenge for any hierarchy, whether it is functional, product, or geographic, is diversity. This is because the scarcest resource in an organization is general management time. Figure 2.2 illustrates the situation.

The team at the top of any hierarchy has only so much time for absorbing information, communicating among themselves and others, and deciding upon actions to take. Business strategies involving a single product to a single market segment give management enough time to concentrate on the flow of orders in—and the flow of products out—of the company. They can synchronize and integrate functions effectively around these flows.

When business strategies call for multiple products going to multiple market segments, the general management time required exceeds that which is available. Management must make many decisions about priorities for allocating functional resources to different products and different markets. Information must be processed about these different products in different markets. In order to see that decisions are made to respond to changes, management must either split the business

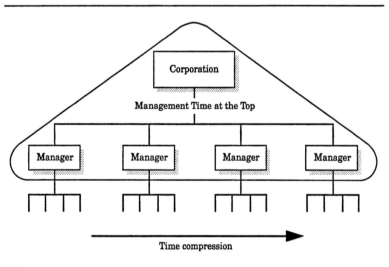

Figure 2.2
General Organization Hierarchy

unit into two or more functional business units of less diversity, or decentralize through some form of lateral organization (Galbraith, 1977). It is the latter course that it is of interest in this book. The greater the amount of diversity of products/services and market segments, the greater the need for lateral coordination across functions. Business teams and other forms of lateral organization are one of the primary means for providing the lateral coordination.

Another enemy of hierarchy is change. General management teams arrive at decisions about allocations of budgets and people to new product programs. They set milestones and introduction dates. Inevitably something unforeseen happens, which requires changes in schedules and priorities. General management must then re-learn the situation, re-decide allocations and milestones, and re-communicate to all affected parties. Thus, the greater the uncertainty and number of unanticipated changes, the greater the amount of information processing and decision-making at the top of the hierarchy (Galbraith, 1977). Like diversity, the greater the amount of uncertainty and unanticipated change that a business unit experiences, the greater the need for lateral coordination and usage of lateral organizational forms.

A third feature that consumes top-management time is the interdependence of cross-departmental work. In functional manufacturing organizations, a serial interdependence is caused by the flow of orders and products across the functions. These flows need to be sequentially coordinated. If there is only one product, top management can provide the coordination. But if there are several products and numerous exceptions, interdependence will need to be managed through lateral coordination. The impact of interdependence can be illustrated by comparing service organizations with manufacturing organizations. Boeing is using roughly 250 teams to perform the design and manufacture of the 777 aircraft. Some teams are created around sections of the aircraft, like the wing, avionics, cockpit, and engines. Some are created to serve customers, such as United and British Airways. All of these teams are interdependent because they are designing a single aircraft. That design needs to be tightly integrated. Therefore, the teams performing the design must be tightly integrated and coordinated. A great deal of communication across teams and up and down the hierarchy is required to resolve the many design conflicts and yet maintain the integrity of the airplane design.

A service company may also be using 250 teams to conduct its work. An investment bank or consulting firm may be using teams for deals or projects for 250 different clients. Each of these teams is independent of the others. They can conduct their business without communicating extensively across teams or up and down the hierarchy. There are far fewer design conflicts to be resolved. Top management is not intimately involved with day-to-day decisions. Thus, less interdependence requires far less communication and coordination.

Since the 1980s, two strategic initiatives have been undertaken by many organizations. These are Total Quality and Time Based Competition. Both of these initiatives are creating the need for much more cross-functional coordination, hence greater lateral organization. Both initiatives increase the interdependence between functions. Total Quality focuses all functions on quality as defined by the customer. Each function has a customer, either internal or external, and defines quality as meeting that customer's needs. Implementation inevitably leads to a focus on management processes that cut across functional boundaries. Thus, Total Quality is inherently a lateral process requiring cross-functional coordination.

However, it is the Time Based initiatives that really require tight and total coordination across functions (Stalk and Hout, 1991). More and more companies are reducing the time it takes to fill a customer order, to produce the product, to process an invoice, to move cash along the value-added chain, or to introduce a new product. Heretofore, organizations separated functions with buffers, such as in-process inventories, and smoothed work flows with order backlogs and delays (see Galbraith, 1977, Chapter 6). Once these buffers are removed, sequential functional operations must balance capacities, synchronize activities, and respond immediately to a defect or failure. The interdependence between functions has increased enormously. Decisions concerning changes cannot wait while the issue is referred to top management for consideration. Instead, decisions have to be decentralized to the lateral organization for quick resolution.

Thus, there are five forces that create a need for lateral coordination across functions within a business unit. These forces are listed in Table 2.2. The greater the diversity and variety in a

Table 2.2
Factors Forcing Cross-Functional Communication

1. Diversity or Variety

2. Unanticipated Changes

3. Work Interdependence

4. Total Quality Initiatives

5. Time Compression

company's products and markets, the greater the need for lateral coordination between functions. The greater the number of unanticipated changes, the greater the need for lateral coordination. The greater the interdependence of work units, the greater the need for communication and lateral coordination. If the company is pursuing Total Quality initiatives, it will have a greater need for lateral coordination. Finally, most of all, the shorter the time cycles, the greater the need for lateral coordination. It is unlikely that the hierarchy alone can provide this coordination. Instead, the organization will need a lateral organizational capability for managing these business forces.

2. Corporate or Cross-Profit Center Coordination

The next type of lateral coordination is that which takes place across business units, or profit centers, within the corporation. Often there are business opportunities for two or more business units to exploit jointly. In addition, there are numerous occasions within functions and across the corporation to share resources, experiences, and best practices. The frequency with which these opportunities arise—and their potential payoff— varies with the corporate strategy of the company.

In the past, corporate strategies were divided into three pure types, as shown in Table 2.3. For each strategy there was an appropriate form of organizational structure (Galbraith, 1993). The single-business strategy of an Apple Computer or Wrigley Chewing Gum was implemented through a functional structure. This single-profit-center type of business requires lateral coordination across functions and across countries, but not across businesses. Our interest in this section is in the two

Table 2.3
Corporate Strategies and Structures

Strategy	Single Business	Multiple Related Businesses	Multiple Unrelated Businesses
Structure	Functional	Divisional	Holding Company

diversified types, multiple related businesses and multiple unrelated businesses. For those companies that diversified into related businesses, such as Procter & Gamble, the multidivisional profit-center type was the appropriate structure. This structure was characterized by moderate decentralization to divisions (usually called business units) and active, large (numbering in the thousands) corporate staffs. Most coordination across business units was accomplished through the hierarchy and by the corporate staff. Those companies that diversified (usually by acquisition) into unrelated businesses adopted the holding company or conglomerate structure. This structure is characterized by almost complete decentralization to business units and small (numbering in the hundreds) staffs. Since the business units were unrelated, there was little opportunity for payoff from cross-business-unit cooperation. Therefore, coordination across business units was not even pursued or suggested. Thus, neither of the above strategy/structure types made lateral organization a high priority.

The situation has changed considerably. Both types of organizations are changing by becoming more like each other and finding that they need lateral coordination. The result is a continuum, shown in Fig. 2.3. The classical types of structure are on the extremes of the continuum, with most organizations somewhere in between (see Galbraith, 1993). Several well-known corporations are placed along the continuum for reference. The continuum conveys variation in the portfolio strategy of the corporation. The strategy consists of two related factors: the diversity of businesses in the portfolio and the amount of value that the corporation adds to the businesses.

The diversity of the business portfolio, as measured by the number of standard industry classification (SIC) codes in which

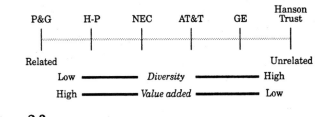

Figure 2.3
Continuum of Corporate Strategies

they participate, varies from low for Procter & Gamble to high for British conglomerate Hanson Trust. The other dimension shown is how much value the corporation adds to a business unit. If a business unit is a stand-alone company, it receives no value from a parent corporation. If, on the other hand, it is a business unit under a corporate umbrella, it has a privileged access to the corporation's resources and proprietary know-how. The less diverse the corporation, the more resources and knowledge can be shared, and the more value a corporation can add to a business that is related to the others in its portfolio. For diverse, unrelated businesses, little value is added except access to financial resources and knowledge. While little value is added, little overhead is charged to a business unit in a holding company. All types of strategies are viable as long as the appropriate organization is chosen for the strategy.

There are several reasons why divisionalized companies are becoming more like holding companies. The first is that divisionalized companies are decentralizing more decisions to their business units. More policy freedom is being given to the businesses in order for them to be more competitive in their market rather than be common across the company. The business unit will use competitors and industry practice as a reference for policies, rather than the corporate way of doing things. AT&T has literally torn its business units apart by vertically disintegrating and decentralizing decisions. Its long-distance business competes with MCI, its switching business competes with such global giants as Siemens and NEC, and its consumer business competes with Japanese and other Asian consumer electronics companies. Thus AT&T and, since 1992, IBM have differentiated their business units from each other, decentralized corporate staffs to the businesses, and given them more freedom of action. AT&T has moved from a divisionalized company to a diversified corporation, but is short of being a holding company.

The holding companies have been moving the other way. ITT, Rockwell, and United Technologies have been reducing the number of businesses in their portfolios. In general, diversified companies have been reducing the number of businesses and increasing the number of countries in which they operate. The break-up of the conglomerates has been initiated by the financial community, which does not value diversification for the purpose of diversifying a portfolio; they believe investors can diversify their own portfolios. They also believe that conglomerates have been under-performers. Despite the lack of evidence for that belief (Grant et al., 1988), conglomerates trade at a lower stock price/earnings ratio. Therefore, the conglomerate either breaks itself apart or an unfriendly investor will do it for them. What is more, the financial markets want to know how the company will make a business more valuable as a member of its portfolio versus the business as a separate company. Therefore ITT, TRW, and other former conglomerates are becoming more like divisionalized companies. They require a more active corporate unit to add value. But no matter where a corporation is located on the continuum, there is a demand that the corporation add more value to a business than it charges in overhead.

Adding value has become the basis for determining the corporate strategy. And the more value and the more types of value a corporation adds to its businesses, the more lateral coordination will be needed among the businesses. There are at least three reasons for the need for lateral organization across businesses in a corporation. The first is the disappearance and transformation of the corporate staff (Lawler and Galbraith, 1993). Corporate staffs have been greatly reduced in number and altered in scope as a result of cost pressures, substituting information technology, recognizing more business diversity (as AT&T did), contracting out, and decentralization. Their new role is actually the old role of advice, service, and strategic support (Fayol, 1925). The staff also become designers and orchestrators of the lateral organization across businesses and subsidiaries.

Therefore, the lateral organization must take over the lateral coordination task from the reduced staff.

The second reason is the shifting of competition and competitive advantage to capabilities (Prahalad and Hammel, 1990; Stalk et al., 1992; Grant, 1991). As virtually every phenomenon goes digital and new materials are fabricated or bio-engineered, industries are constantly in flux. Markets and industries are hard to define. New competitors playing under different rules emerge. Kodak now finds itself competing with Canon and Sony as well as Fuji. The product no longer is photography, it is "imaging" now. The definition of business units needs to be flexible as products, markets, industries, and competitors constantly change. Companies instead focus on capabilities, such as electronic color imaging for Kodak. Kodak wants to become a world color standard, as Dolby is for sound. This capability is to be built and shared by a number of business units. Capabilities are more stable and provide a long-run framework for investing and competing. Capabilities and the people associated with them belong to the corporation, not the business unit. People and information need to be shared across business units. Capability building and sharing require lateral coordination.

The third reason for lateral organization is the increasing opportunity for *internal* joint ventures among business units. The increasing investments in R&D and intangible assets mean that not even huge companies like IBM can afford to develop and maintain capabilities in all technologies and skills. One response has been the creation of numerous joint ventures to share and build technologies (Mytelka, 1991). There are also opportunities—as well as the necessity—for building and sharing capabilities inside the corporation. Discovering and managing of these opportunities requires lateral coordination and lateral organization.

Another set of opportunities for internal joint ventures arises because of the flux in markets and industries. It is difficult to define business-unit boundaries. Often, two or more business units can combine capabilities and address a newly emerging market or change an existing one. Restructuring industries create many opportunities for the multibusiness corporation. When combined with the strong financial resources of many diversified companies, there are many opportunities to develop new businesses inside of the corporation through joint ventures, mergers, and restructuring. The corporation with an effective lateral organization will be in a good position to recognize and act upon these opportunities.

Western companies in general, and American companies in particular, have been very unsuccessful in working across business units. As a result, there are many missed opportunities waiting for those companies that can develop a lateral capability to surface them. Even if there were no new opportunities created by industry restructuring, companies could profit from lateral coordination across business units. Thus, existing missed opportunities, new opportunities created by emerging industries and markets, and the necessity to partner with someone to share R&D investments will create an advantage for the company that can address these opportunities through its lateral organization.

Thus several factors are combining to create a need for lateral coordination across business units. Corporations are all looking for ways to add value to businesses. The corporate staffs that used to perform some of the value-adding activities are disappearing. Unique capabilities are becoming one way to add value to all businesses. As a result, competition is centering on capabilities that are distributed among the business units. In addition, the same forces creating partnerships and alliances between companies are creating opportunities for partnering inside the corporation. Real, tangible benefits will accrue to the corporation that can coordinate across business units to create the internal partnerships.

3. International or Cross-Subsidiary Coordination

The last form of lateral coordination takes place across and within geographic units. Companies have found that it is impossible to find a single comprehensive organization structure that will coordinate all of their international activities (Bartlett, 1983). Inevitably, the company must employ lateral coordination across countries within a business unit, and across business units within a country. How much coordination is needed will vary with the international strategy of the company.

The international strategy of a company varies along two dimensions (Porter, 1986; Prahalad and Doz, 1987; Bartlett and Ghoshal, 1989). The first is the degree to which a business pursues a single, globally integrated strategy around the world. The second is the degree to which value-adding activities are dispersed around the world. Both of these strategic dimensions can vary from a minimal amount to a great deal. They are shown schematically in Fig. 2.4 as global integration and global dispersion. Figure 2.4 shows the four possible strategies that can result. In the next sections, the global dimensions will be discussed, along with the factors that cause them to be either high or low. The section proceeds by first explaining global integration and global dispersion. There are several factors that are causing managers to choose more of both of these dimensions. Then, each of the four categories illustrated by the four boxes in Fig. 2.4 will be explained.

Global Integration. Businesses vary considerably in their need to formulate and execute their strategy on a globally integrated basis. One business may be very local and may have little need to integrate strategy across countries or regions. In such a case, the international strategy for the business simply results from an accumulation of independently determined coun-

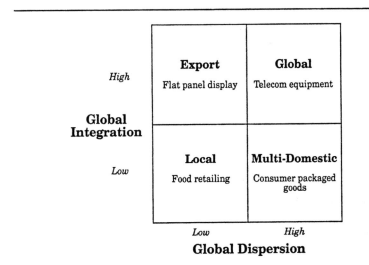

Figure 2.4
Dimensions of Global Strategy

try strategies for the business. The company may do business in many countries, but in each country it can formulate its strategy independently of the other countries.

Other businesses must formulate their strategies with a great deal of coordination and integration across countries. When Hewlett-Packard introduced its Spectrum Series of computers (its RISC architecture product), they invested $400 million in R&D and another $400 million in plant, equipment, and working capital. With fixed costs of $800 million, H-P must rely on sales from around the world to recover these costs. Because they cannot generate enough volume in the United States alone to pay for the investment, the product strategy and design must be coordinated across all countries. The product must be designed from the beginning to run French software and give error messages in Kanji characters for Asia. There must be common sales and service policies for Mitsubishi Trading Company, which will purchase systems for its Tokyo, New York, Singapore, and London offices. In the computer business, countries cannot formulate independent strategies. Country subsidiaries must collectively formulate and execute globally integrated product strategies.

The degree of global integration required will therefore vary with the nature of the business. There are several factors that will determine the amount of integration that is needed within a business across countries. These factors are listed in Table 2.4, and are explained in the following sections.

1. Proportion of Fixed Costs. When there are substantial fixed costs in a business, as in the Hewlett-Packard example, the company cannot rely on domestic volume alone to recover them. Therefore, the business requires global volume,

Table 2.4
Factors Causing Global Business Integration

1. High Proportion of Fixed Costs

2. Homogeneous Markets and Universal Products

3. Global Customers and Competitors

along with globally integrated strategies and plans to achieve that volume. One measure of fixed costs is percent of sales reinvested in R&D. Electronics, computers, semiconductors, and pharmaceuticals, which invest 10 percent, 12 percent, and 15 percent of sales in R&D, are all businesses that require global volume to cover high fixed R&D costs. They cannot afford to duplicate R&D efforts in North America, Europe, and East Asia. On the other hand, some consumer packaged goods and major home-appliance businesses invest about 1–2 percent of sales in R&D. There is much less need to plan product strategy on a globally integrated basis in these businesses.

Another measure is the percent of sales reinvested in fixed assets. Capital-intensive businesses are more global than low-fixed-asset businesses, other factors being the same. Again, there is a need for volume that exceeds that of the domestic economy. Semiconductors is again a good example. In addition to heavy R&D investment, there are enormous investments in silicon-fabrication facilities and equipment. For the next generations of dynamic random access memories (DRAMs), the fixed costs approach a billion dollars for the R&D and another billion dollars for plant and equipment. Clearly, product and investment strategies must be planned and executed on a globally integrated basis.

Similar situations arise for service businesses investing heavily in information technology. Investments in worldwide telecommunications networks, local area networks, software, and databases are increasing the need for a global volume of transactions. Citibank and Chase need to plan some of their businesses, such as credit cards, on a globally integrated basis.

2. Products and Markets. A second factor pertains to the products and markets of the business. To the degree that markets are homogeneous across countries, universal products can be designed for them, thereby achieving the scale needed to cover fixed costs. Again, businesses vary in market homogeneity and product universality. In some businesses, markets homogenized across countries in the 1980s. Consumer buying habits were driven more by disposable income, education, and exposure to global media than by nationality. Products such as Sharp calculators, Seiko watches, and the Sony Walkman were the same all over the world. On the other hand, the size and function of refrigerators varies considerably around the world. Different countries exhibit different food preferences, different shopping habits, and different sizes of homes. The market for home appliances is heterogeneous, and products are locally differentiated, not universal. In summary, a globally integrated business is one that has high fixed costs, produces universal products or services, and serves homogeneous markets around the world. At the other extreme is a local business with low fixed costs and heterogeneous markets around the world that are served with a great deal of product variety.

3. Customers and Competitors. The last factor determining the degree to which a business requires a globally coordinated strategy is the nature of the customers and competitors. If the customers to which a company sells and the competitors with which it vies are themselves global, then the business requires a global strategy. On the other hand, if the customers and competitors are different in every region of the world, the business is best addressed through a number of independently generated local strategies. Most businesses will be characterized by mixtures of global and local customers and competitors. But the greater the proportion of global customers (who shop globally) and competitors, the greater the need for a coordinated business strategy worldwide.

In summary, there is a continuum ranging from the need for a single, globally integrated business strategy to the need for a collection of independently generated local strategies. The globally integrated strategy is required when facing global competitors in businesses with high fixed costs, selling universally standard products to homogeneous markets consisting of global customers. A local strategy is required in the exact opposite situation.

Global Dispersion. The second dimension of international strategy that has consequences for lateral coordination is the degree to which a company has dispersed its activities around the world. Dispersion has two aspects to it. One is simply the number of countries in which a company does business. The second is the amount of value that is added in a country. It is possible to do business in many countries but have only a sales office in each of them. The real organizational issues arise when service, manufacturing, and R&D are located in many countries. It is the combination of a large number of countries and numerous value-adding activities in those countries that generates the need for lateral coordination.

Global dispersion, like global integration, varies for different businesses and different countries. The factors that influence global dispersion are listed in Table 2.5.

1. Active Local Governments. Local governments vary in the degree to which they demand value added in their country as a quid pro quo for access to their country's market. The strength of the demands varies with the political ideology of the country and the attractiveness of its markets. Countries with state-owned enterprises and large populations—for example, China and Indonesia—can be very demanding.

In the future, all governments will be more demanding; the bargaining power is going their way. First of all, companies need access to all markets to get global volume. Their increasing investments in R&D and other intangibles are raising their fixed costs. To get access to country markets, companies will have to invest and add value in that country. Second, almost all countries are following Japan's example of export-led economic growth. But where are all those exports going to go? They used to go to the United States, which kept its markets reasonably open. Now the United States needs exports, too. Some predict that in the future market access will become the scarcest, most desired commodity (Thurow, 1992).

2. Search for the Best Site. Companies would disperse their activities even if there were no demands coming from local

Table 2.5
Factors Causing Global Dispersion

1. Active Local Governments

2. Search for the Best Location
   - Manufacturing
   - Product Development, R&D
   - Headquarters

governments. Competitive forces cause companies to search the world for the best location for a particular activity. Initially, the search was for low labor costs for unskilled jobs. This search continues as companies locate and relocate manufacturing plants in the lowest-cost sites. The uncertainty associated with political instability and unpredictable exchange and wage rates is causing companies to use several factory locations. They use a portfolio of producing sites as a hedge against uncertainty. The use of a portfolio increases the dispersion of a company's activities.

The new search is for the best site for highly skilled people. In today's competitive environment, a company needs the best skills available, and it will search the world for them. The increasing use of telecommunications allows the company to integrate an activity into its operations independent of its physical location.

And, finally, companies are moving their business headquarters out of the country of company ownership to the best worldwide location. Typically, a headquarters is moved to a country where the toughest competitors and most demanding customers are located. These countries provide the advanced markets that will drive the direction of competition in the future.

It is the search for the best location and demands of local governments that cause companies to locate activities in different countries. Both of these factors are likely to increase, thereby increasing both the number of countries in which to do business and the number of value-adding activities in those countries. These topics will be presented in more depth in Chapter 6.

Types of International Strategies

The two dimensions of international strategy can now be combined into four types of strategies. These strategic types are important, because it is the combination of global integration and global dispersion that generates the need for lateral coordination.

1. Local Strategy. The least interesting businesses, from an international point of view, are those that require neither global integration nor global dispersion. Food retailing is an example. In the United States, it is not even a national business.

2. Export Strategy. Some companies participate in businesses that require global integration, but concentrate all of their activities in the home country. Boeing, for example, participates in a globally integrated business, but concentrates its activities around the Seattle area and exports its product. Japanese industry, until the mid-1980s, concentrated all manufacturing, procurement, product development, and R&D in Japan and exported from there. The only activities in other countries were sales offices, distribution, after-sales service, and local marketing. The bulk of the value-adding activities were concentrated in Japan. The flat-panel display business is still characterized by a heavy concentration of value-adding activities in Japan. These businesses follow an international strategy of *export.*

3. Multi-Domestic Strategy. Some companies have dispersed their activities around the world, but participate in businesses that require little effort to integrate these activities. The consumer packaged-goods industry in general, and Nestlé specifically, are good examples of this strategy. The packaged food products manufactured by Nestlé vary considerably with national tastes. The customers are all local retailers, and distribution varies widely. There is low investment in R&D; the business simply does not need to be integrated across the heterogeneous markets.

Nestlé is located in over 160 countries and manufactures in most of them. From a dispersion point of view, Nestlé is a global company. But from an integration perspective, it is a collection of country subsidiaries. Its international strategy is called *multi-domestic.* Instead of a single, integrated global strategy, Nestlé's international strategy is a collection of independent, domestic strategies. As a result, there has been little need for lateral integration across country subsidiaries.

4. Global Strategy. The last and most challenging category of business is that which is globally dispersed yet requires a high degree of global business integration. This international strategy is defined as *global.* The computer and telecommunications businesses are typical of this category. Ericson, AT&T, and Fijitsu are all challenged with coordination requirements of this truly global type of business. The R&D, training, and software investments are in the multi-billion-dollar range. The costs to develop and deliver the next generation of fiber-optic and digital telecommunications switch will be an investment of several billion dollars. Thus, AT&T, NEC, and Siemens must all from the beginning design their switches to be modifiable to sell in North America, Europe, and Asia. The subsidiaries of these companies must jointly plan and execute the product design. Telecom is a business that requires a globally integrated strategy.

On the other hand, the switches are purchased by regulated and state-owned telephone companies. These are local companies which require unique changes in the switches to work in their network. The governments usually require some value added in their country as a condition for purchase. Therefore, the telecom companies must locate sales, after-sales service, software engineers, manufacturing, and product design people in each major market. The value-adding activities of the large telecom companies are thereby globally dispersed. These companies require global integration as well as global dispersion. These are the truly global companies.

In summary, the international strategies of companies vary in their requirements for global integration and global dispersion. In combination, these requirements determine the amount of lateral coordination. Either factor by itself poses minimal international coordination requirements. Indeed, Nestlé's international businesses were created at a time when managers traveled by boat and communicated by letter. Japan's exporters had extremely difficult cross-functional coordination challenges but minimal international ones. Their products were designed, manufactured, tested, and shipped from Japan. Participants in the process were all local Japanese or Japanese expatriates.

It is the combination of requirements for integration and dispersion that creates the need for lateral coordination. It is when participants in the strategy formulation and execution process are geographically dispersed, face different market requirements, reside in different time zones, and often speak different languages that organization designers face their greatest challenge.

Three Different Capabilities

The previous sections described three different types of lateral coordination which are needed in different parts of the organization. They are discussed together in this book because the design logic for creating the lateral organization is the same for all three types. But it is also important to note that the three types represent three different capabilities. Being good at one type does not ensure being good at the other types. Many American corporations are good at coordinating products across functions in a business unit. At the same time, they are ineffective in coordinating across business units. The reason is that the capability must be created by aligning all of the organizational elements shown in the Star Model (Fig. 1.1) at the appropriate levels and places within the organization. The fact that a company has aligned structures, processes, rewards and measurements, and human resource practices within a business unit does not necessarily mean that the alignment has been built across businesses at the corporate level. So even if the lateral organization concepts are the same for all three types of coordination, the alignment must be built in each part of the organization where they will be applied.

Summary

This chapter has described three types of lateral coordination: (1) across functions within a business unit, (2) across business units within the corporation, (3) across countries within a business unit and the corporation. The chapter also described the forces that are increasing the priority of capabilities to coordinate these activities with the lateral organization. It also pointed out that strategies vary in their need for lateral coordination; lateral coordination is much more important to some strategies than to others. The coordination requirements vary as follows:

1. Across functions within a business unit, the greater the amount of product and market diversity, the greater the need for lateral cross-functional coordination. The shorter the time cycles in the business, the greater the need for lateral coordination.

2. Across business units within a corporation, the less the diversity in the corporate portfolio of businesses and the greater the types and amounts of value added to the businesses, the greater the need for cross-business, lateral coordination.

3. Across countries within a business unit, the greater the amount of global integration and global dispersion, the greater the need for cross-country, lateral coordination.

In all cases, different strategies lead to different types and amounts of lateral coordination.

The next chapters will describe the varying types and amounts of lateral organization. These variations are to be matched with the varying amounts of lateral coordination that follow from the different strategies for business units, international activities, and the corporation.

3

Lateral Organization

The previous chapters have argued that competition is increasingly taking place around capabilities. Among these capabilities are the organizational capabilities to execute difficult tasks. The organizational capability of interest in this book is the execution of tasks that require coordination among organizational units. The last chapter explained the variety of situations in which this lateral coordination capability could be applied. The point was also made that different strategies require different amounts of lateral coordination. In turn, different amounts of lateral coordination lead to different amounts and types of lateral organization. This chapter describes these different types of lateral organization and presents the first type—the informal, voluntary organization.

Lateral Organizational Types

Chapter 1 defined the lateral organization as a mechanism for the decentralization of general management decisions to a group of people from different organizational units that are affected by an issue. This lateral organization is used when it results in decisions that are faster and superior to those that the general manager could make. It is faster and superior when there are a large number of cross-organizational decisions to be made. Chapter 2 described the kinds of strategies that, when implemented, create many of these cross-organizational issues. The task of the organization designer is to create the types and amounts of lateral organization that are commensurate with the lateral coordination requirements of the strategy.

The reason for matching the lateral organization to the strategy is that lateral organization comes at a cost. As mentioned in Chapter 1, lateral organization requires an investment of time communicating, deciding, and resolving conflicts. The matching is facilitated by the different types of lateral organization and the different amounts that can be applied. The three basic types of lateral organization vary in the amount of management time they require. They also vary in the amount of difficulty experienced in implementing them. The three basic types are listed in Fig. 3.1, along with the different amounts that can be applied.

The first type, the voluntary organization, is the simplest and easiest to use. It is also the least expensive. The further down the list the organization proceeds, the more difficult and more expensive the forms of lateral organization become. Therefore, the designer should proceed down the list, adding more lateral organization, only to the point where the costs of organization match the benefits of coordination. Thus, each category of lateral organization down the list is more complex and more expensive than the one above it. The next section explains why.

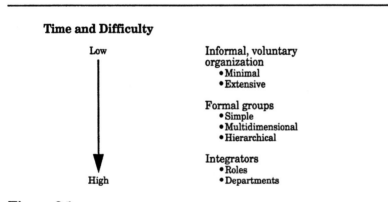

Figure 3.1
Types and Amounts of Lateral Organization

1. *Voluntary Organization*

The simplest lateral organization—and the one easiest to use—is the informal organization. It is a voluntary organization because it is formed at the initiation of those comprising it. The managers perceive a situation and spontaneously communicate among themselves to resolve the issue. Top management may be informed, but is otherwise not directly involved. Hence, the collective action is informal, yet it is organized. This voluntary organization may be minimal in scope or extensive. The scope will depend on the lateral coordination requirements of the strategy. At investment banks, for example, which implement many fast-moving deals for many clients, it is extensive (Eccles and Crane, 1988).

2. *Formal Groups*

If the coordination requirements of the strategy can be met by using only the voluntary organization, the organization designer should not use any of the more complicated forms. Any additional lateral mechanisms will unnecessarily complicate decision-making and raise costs. On the other hand, many strategies do require the additional decision-making capacity provided by formal groups. In order to guarantee coordination and increase accountability, top management may create a group to act in some capacity, such as a product team. Because the informal organization may not spontaneously arise for every company need, some formal or top management-created groups will be required.

The formal groups usually have a name applied to them, such as a board, council, or team, and they usually require more work. Since the formal group did not form voluntarily, some effort is usually required to get the members to work as a team. Formal groups have more difficulty functioning effectively. They are less natural than voluntary groups, and thus are more costly and require more time and effort to maintain.

A second reason that formal groups are more costly is that they are used in addition to the voluntary group, not in place of it. The use of lateral mechanisms is a cumulative process. As a more complicated form is added, the simpler forms are not abandoned. They are still needed, but are insufficient by themselves to achieve the time-to-market or global integration required by the strategy. The organization needs to make more decisions more often. It needs both the informal and formal groups to supplement the general manager. Thus the organization designer adds more complicated forms, to the point where the desired coordination is achieved. To use less complicated forms than called for would fail to implement the strategy. To use more complicated forms than called for would be to incur unnecessary costs and complications.

The use of formal groups can also vary from a few to many groups, depending on the strategy. The groups can also vary from simple (one-dimensional) to multidimensional. For example, a consumer goods company can be organized around country and regional profit centers. It may employ five global product teams to coordinate its R&D investments. In this case, the groups are few (5) and simple (based on a single dimension of products). At the opposite end of the spectrum are the design/build teams used by Boeing on its 777 program. These teams are formed around sections of the aircraft, customers, and technologies. The groups are many (250) and multidimensional. The coordination requirements and lateral coordination costs are much higher on the 777 program.

In addition to being multidimensional, formal groups can also be hierarchical. An organization may form several customer groups. Each group may want something very different for its customer. A steering group may resolve cross-customer-group conflicts, by balancing responsiveness and duplication costs. Thus the use of teams can vary from a few simple ones to many multidimensional and hierarchical ones. The task of the organizational designer is to match the requirements of the strategy to the extensiveness of the types of lateral organization. The design of groups, both simple and multidimensional, is addressed in Chapter 4.

3. Integrators

The integrating role is the third and most complex form of lateral organization. At some point, the groups require some full-time leadership. In order to achieve time-to-market, the product teams will probably require a full-time new product manager to convene the groups and resolve cross-unit conflicts. These leaders are referred to as integrators (Lawrence and Lorsch, 1967). They often have titles such as project manager, program manager, product manager, worldwide business manager, and brand manager. They have in common two features: First, they are all "little general managers," managing a portion of the general manager's accountabilities. They are necessary when the number of decisions required by the strategy demands more general manager decision capacity. The general manager's role is then divided and delegated to several little general managers. These integrators will also guide the lateral groups in their activities. The second feature is that integrators execute their role without any formal authority. The authority resides in the line organization.

The task of the organization designer when creating integrating roles is twofold. First, there must be a process for developing and selecting people who can influence without authority. And second, there are additional power bases that can be created to augment the personal skills of the integrator. Both of these issues must be addressed in order to successfully implement the integrator role. These issues are discussed in Chapter 5.

The implementation of the integrating role is the most expensive and the most difficult of the lateral forms of organization. It is most expensive because it involves hiring a group of people whose sole task is to integrate the work of other people. When information is needed, there may even be integrating departments created. This cost is incurred in addition to the cost of voluntary and formal groups of various types. The cost is an investment in management. The investment is to achieve time-to-market, global integration, or value added. These strategic goals cannot be achieved by the hierarchy acting alone. The investment is to give the organization the capability of acting multidimensionally.

The integrating role is the most difficult form to execute because of the conflicts it generates. The organization consists of managers from two dimensions. In the international company, people represent businesses and geographies. Each one will see the situations differently, and conflicts will result. Top management needs to adopt a conflict-resolution process that resolves these inevitable conflicts on a timely basis and in the interests of the company. This type of decision process is difficult to create.

The companies that can create one will have a significant advantage over competitors.

In summary, the lateral forms represent a cumulative commitment to lateral coordination. Simple situations will require only an informal, lateral organization. If satisfactory results can be achieved by using the simple form, the organization should stop at the voluntary organization. Other strategies will require formal groups in addition to the informal, spontaneous organization. And, finally, integrators may be required to act as leaders of the lateral groups, both formal and informal. Integrators are the most costly and difficult of the different types of lateral organization. However, they are required for the most demanding strategic tasks, such as compressed time cycles and global integration.

Matching Lateral Coordination and Organization

The position that has been developed up to this point is summarized in Table 3.1. The basic premise is that different strategies require different amounts of lateral coordination. To achieve the lateral coordination, different types and amounts of lateral organization are required. For business units, greater cross-functional coordination is required for strategies pursuing multiple products or services delivered to multiple customer segments. Business units following strategies of continuously reduced cycle times will require more lateral coordination than those conducting business at a normal pace. The pursuit of diversity and speed will require more types and amounts of lateral coordination across functions within a business. Those businesses trying to deliver multiple products rapidly to multiple customers will utilize product teams, customer teams, and product managers, in addition to function managers.

The basic premise is best illustrated by the work of Lawrence and Lorsch (1967). They compared the types and amounts of lateral organization that were used in three different industries. They selected the most effective company in the industry to serve as the example. The industries varied in the degree to which new product development was the basis of competition. The container industry was the most stable, showing that new products account for zero percent of the revenue. In the

Table 3.1
Strategies Requiring Increasing Lateral Coordination and Lateral Organization

Business Strategy	Corporate Strategy	International Strategy	Lateral Organization
Low Diversity/ Slow Speed	High Diversity/ Low Value Added	Low Global Integration and Dispersion	Informal Organization
			↓
			Formal Groups
↓	↓	↓	↓
High Diversity/ Fast Speed	Low Diversity High Value Added	High Global Integration and Dispersion	Integrators

food industry, 15 percent of the revenue came from new products, while the plastics business showed that 35 percent of revenue came from new products. The implication is that companies in the plastics industry require more lateral coordination than the other two industries. Table 3.2 summarizes their findings.

The plastics company does indeed show the use of more types and amounts of lateral organization. It uses voluntary organization, formal groups at three levels, and integrating departments for product management. They employ 22 percent of their managers in integrating roles. The container company provides the contrast. It supplements its normal hierarchical practices with only the informal, voluntary organization. Recall that this company was the most effective in its industry. The conclusion is that companies should use only as much lateral organization as is necessary. The coordination requirements of the strategy are the factor that determines what is necessary. As companies in the food and plastics industries follow strategies of competing in new products, they must add lateral organization to implement that strategy. The more new product activity, the greater the investment in lateral organization.

The corporation is the second area of lateral coordination. Again, different corporate strategies require different amounts of lateral coordination. The portfolio strategies of some conglomerates add little value other than financial value to a diverse set of businesses; these require little cross-business-unit coordination. On the other hand, companies contributing significant value to multiple related businesses will require substantial coordination across those businesses. Informal relations, technology councils, and global account managers will be used to execute the latter strategies. Intermediate strategies will require lesser amounts of lateral organization.

Multinational, multi-business companies have a similar set of issues. Those companies that follow strategies requiring small amounts of global integration and global dispersion will require little lateral coordination across countries. On the other hand, certain companies pursue global strategies that require a great deal of integration across countries, using geographically dispersed activities; these companies will require a great deal of lateral coordination. These companies will require coordination within a business and across countries, as well as within a coun-

Table 3.2
Matching Strategy and Organization

	Plastics	Food	Container
Percent of Revenue due to New Products	35%	15%	0%
Coordination	Hierarchy	Hierarchy	Hierarchy
Mechanisms Used	Voluntary	Voluntary	Voluntary
	Formal Groups at 3 Levels	Formal Groups	—
	Integrating Departments	Integrating Roles	—
Percent Integrators/Managers	22%	17%	0%

try across businesses. In addition to informal relationships, these latter multinationals will require country teams with business representation, business teams with country representation, and business and country managers. They must commit to a substantial amount of lateral organization.

The point in each of these cases is that different strategies lead to different types and amounts of lateral organization. In order to effectively implement a strategy, the organization designer must match the types and amounts of lateral organization that are commensurate with the requirements of that strategy. In order to achieve a match, the designer must understand the coordination needs of different strategies and match different organizations to the different coordination needs.

The next chapters detail the three basic types of lateral organization, with the remainder of this chapter dedicated to the voluntary and informal organization. Chapter 4 presents the design of formal groups, and Chapter 5 describes the issues in designing organizations for the successful use of integrating roles.

The Informal Organization

A great deal of interdepartmental activity that takes place in the organization is spontaneous and voluntary. Two or a few people confront an issue and resolve it among themselves. In this manner, the organization experiences unplanned decentralization; that is, an unanticipated event occurs, and the people closest to it marshal the resources to deal with it. This kind of voluntary behavior is usually referred to as the informal organization. These acts occur hundreds of times per day in an organization and can be a great source of strength. They can speed work and response time to customers and suppliers. It can be a weakness when they do not occur naturally, when people do not act spontaneously or cooperatively. The informal organization is well known and documented, but what is new are the attempts to facilitate its formation in pursuit of organizational goals.

By definition, the informal organization connotes something that just happens. Because it is spontaneous and voluntary, it is assumed to be random and uncontrollable. Today, however, many organizations also see it as subject to design and influences. Organization designers can increase the odds that voluntary contacts will occur, and that they will occur in pursuit of organizational goals. This discovery has resulted from recognizing that relationships are created as a by-product of other actions. For example, some companies rotate managers across functions to train them to become general managers. As a by-product, the rotations help those managers build networks of contacts and communication channels that they can use in their day-to-day work. Today, the by-product, voluntary communication, is becoming as desirable as the primary product, personal development. If a company can achieve both results from the same experience, it can get effectively two for the price of one.

There are other practices that organizations can use to help build the network of relationships that can form the basis for the voluntary lateral organization. Such practices as interdepartmental rotation, physical location, information technology networks, and interdepartmental events all contribute to the formation of the network. Additional leverage can be obtained if structures across departments mirror each other and if consistent reward and measurement practices are used. Table 3.3 lists the actions that could be taken to increase the probability that people in different departments will naturally and voluntarily communicate, cooperate, and take collective action on an ongoing basis. The result will be a decentralization of cross-departmental or general manager issues.

Table 3.3
Network-Building Practices

Design Actions to Create a Voluntary Lateral Organization

1. Interdepartmental Rotation

2. Physical Location

3. Information Technology Networks

4. Interdepartmental Events

5. Mirror-Image Organizational Structures

6. Consistent Reward and Measurement Practices

Organizational Practices

Informal networks occur naturally, randomly, spontaneously, and voluntarily throughout organizations. Whenever two people with some affinity meet, a relationship is formed. The design of the informal network is simply to eliminate some of the randomness in its creation. The purpose is to increase the probability that *important* relationships are created and used. The organization designer acts as a relationship broker and makes the introductions. Spontaneity and voluntarism reign from then on. Relationships and networks can be created through interdepartmental rotation, co-location, information technology, and interdepartmental events.

1. Interdepartmental Rotation. Rotational assignments are key to building the lateral organizational capability, not just the voluntary organization. Because of this, the rotational process will be addressed in some detail. As mentioned in the previous section, a number of companies use rotational assignments as a management-development tool. When accompanied by supporting practices, rotation can provide a variety of experiences that will help a person acquire the seasoning and perspective required of a general manager. But rotation also builds a network of relationships for the individual and the organization.

There is some evidence supporting the network-building outcome (Galbraith, 1977, pp. 113–114). From communication studies, it is found that managers with interdepartmental experience communicate across departments significantly more often than those managers with no interdepartmental experience. These managers have a larger network and use it on a work-related basis. A second finding is that managers with interdepartmental experience use a more informal means to communicate when they do communicate laterally. They will use a face-to-face discussion or phone call, rather than the memo style favored by less experienced managers.

The reasons for the communication effect are not difficult to understand. Managers who have recently spent two years in sales, for example, are in an excellent position to serve as an interface between their new department and the sales department. These managers know the roles and names of the key players. They know which person to call on which issues. Being familiar with the sales culture and language, they know what to say, how to say it, and what not to say. They have an understanding of the sales position after having "walked in their shoes." In general, rotated managers leave the sales department with knowledge, language, and relationships that can be used to effectively manage the interface between the two departments.

One reason for the informal style used by people who have had interdepartment-rotated experience is that managers who have been rotated are more likely to perceive conflict between departments. Therefore, they approach a contact with more sensitivity and take a more personal approach. Finally, managers with interdepartmental experience are more likely to establish reciprocal relationships. They receive as many contacts as they initiate. Their relationships appear to be beneficial for both parties and are used on an ongoing basis. These results seem to suggest that rotational assignments can increase the amount and quality of cross-departmental communication.

Rotational assignments are effective for all three types of lateral coordination. Cross-functional assignments have been common practice in some organizations. Today, international experience is essential in order to enter the managerial ranks of many companies. Cross-business experience becomes important in the multi-business company. All three types of rotation can result in improved communication and cooperation as well as management development.

The next step is to use rotation as a design tool to improve communication across key interfaces. Often companies are using rotation but not getting the benefit of the lateral organization. One company examined its rotation patterns. It found two rotation paths. One group of managers rotated between sales, marketing, and customer service. Another group rotated between R&D, engineering, and the plants. No one rotated across the two groups. With new efforts at simultaneous engineering, this company needed cross-trained people in engineering and marketing to help reduce time-to-market. By concentrating rotation between key interfaces along workflow paths, relationships will form and aid in cycle-time reductions.

The Royal Dutch Shell company has used international assignments to develop managers for decades. However, they also use it to develop their international organization (Edstrom and Galbraith, 1977). If one examines the top 1000 managers at

Shell, one finds that one third are British, one third are Dutch, and one third are other. The other category includes over 60 nationalities. But what is important is the policy that every country management team will have one nonnational member. These teams all have one expatriate plus others who have had international experience themselves. Indeed, of the top 1000, about one third are currently serving in an expatriate position. Thus there is an extensive network among these people that results in an effective lateral organization and decentralization.

Rotational assignments among a portion of the managerial population are essential to creating a lateral organizational capability. Almost all companies that are effective at lateral organization employ a rotational policy. Dow-Corning has used a well-thought-out approach. Most new members are chemical engineers who enter the product development function. From there they follow their new product into scale-up and then into manufacturing. Once in the factory, they may move to the quality function and then become a controller for the plant. Their careers are across line positions in the functions, as well as between line and staff positions. Next the "engineer" may go to a factory in Europe to be a controller. Each move returns some roles that are familiar while introducing new ones, and the manager is not overwhelmed on any one move. Over time the manager spends time in different functions: in different businesses, in different geographies, and in both line and staff roles. The manager learns to be accountable for results in the line and to influence without authority in the staff. The rotation develops the manager's ability to function in a matrix organization and builds a network of relationships at the same time.

Rotational assignments, despite some excellent examples and success on the part of the Japanese, are still underutilized. There are several reasons for this situation, some valid and some not. The valid reasons revolve around costs. Rotation is not cheap. Shell estimates that on average it costs three times as much to staff a position with an expatriate as with a local. People who rotate are less productive initially because they are still learning and developing. Then, when they become productive, they move on. In a climate of cost containment, companies avoid rotation because of the costs of the program. In addition, there are personal obstacles. The two-career family is a lot less mobile than the single-earner household, and some other people do not want to change location, period.

Some other factors also inhibit rotation. Some companies still have patronage systems in which top managers resist giving up their good people for fear of getting cast-offs in return. In effect, these managers release only the poor performers to the rotation system. In situations where cast-offs have been the rotators, these norms need to be broken and new ones established. Another inhibitor may be the company's compensation system, which penalizes the rotator or does not encourage rotation. Some aspects of this problem can be eliminated by new awareness or skill-based pay systems (Lawler, 1990). These systems pay the person and not the job; the more skills or knowledge a person has, the higher is his or her salary. Lawler finds that 40 percent of U.S. companies are trying some form of person-based salary system. When functioning, such systems encourage lateral movement and learning. With fewer hierarchical levels, lateral progression also becomes more attractive.

There are some alternatives to career moves that commit the manager to several years in another department. Honda rotates its engineers across functions when they join the company. Then they become members of the engineering teams. But Honda has a policy of having engineers spend one week each year working in another department. They spend a week in a dealership, a sales branch, or a purchasing office. In this way, they learn to understand the entire work flow. This experience enables them to compensate for issues in other departments in their daily jobs because they are aware of the consequences of problems that may be caused by their actions. They are also useful in efforts to re-engineer cross-departmental processes and information flows.

A number of high-technology companies (such as Apple Computer) employ sabbaticals. After five years, the employees are given six weeks off to recharge their batteries. Often employees from other departments fill in for the person on sabbatical. In this way, the substitutes can see if they would like a more permanent transfer. But whether they transfer or not, they learn about another department, acquire some department-specific language, and meet new people with whom they establish new relationships.

In summary, interdepartmental experiences lasting from one week to five years can be used for informal network building as well as management development. The two outcomes actually go hand in hand. However, organization designers need to see that rotations occur across key interfaces that require task-related communication. In this way, relationships established during the assignment can become part of the lateral organization. For companies already rotating people, an analysis of the patterns can lead to some improvements in lateral organization at no increase in costs.

2. Physical Co-location. The probability that relationships will be established and used productively between people is partly a function of their proximity. Tom Allen was an early advocate of planning physical location so as to facilitate communication between people and groups (Allen, 1977). Allen's original interest was in co-locating scientists so as to facilitate technology transfer and new ideas in R&D laboratories. However, his research results apply to other work activities as well. The results show clearly that reducing distance and physical barriers between people increases the amount of communication between those people. Therefore, if groups that require cross-unit communication are co-located, the communication process will be facilitated.

Implementation of co-location is not so simple, however. If a product design group is co-located with a manufacturing engineering group, communication between those groups will increase. But communication between the product design group and other engineering groups will decrease. Co-location increases communication with one group and decreases it with others. Co-location is a trade-off decision. Organization designers need to look to the strategy and the work flow for help in making trade-off decisions. If the unit is reducing time-to-market for new products and employing simultaneous engineering, the product design group would be located with the manufacturing people. The designers would look for other mechanisms to link the engineers together. BMW currently employs communications specialists in their organization department to measure communication flows and work flows. Departments are co-located to facilitate work-flow communication.

Airframe manufacturers in the United States have adopted a policy of locating multiple functions working on the same aircraft section in the same building. All design, manufacturing, quality, procurement, and other functions that are working on the wing are located in building 101, the fuselage in 102, the tail section in 103, and so on. Interfunctional groups are located by the section of the aircraft on which they are working. The organization structure is functional, but physical location is by common task. The practice leads to more cross-functional communication and more-effective communication.

Co-location leads to relationships. Engineers and manufacturing people meet each other in the cafeteria, at the coffee machine and copier, or in the restrooms and parking lots. Relationships start with conversations about the Super Bowl, elections, or a new mall in town. Then, when controversial design changes need to be discussed, the participants have a relationship within which a problem-solving dialogue is more likely to happen. Co-location generates more communication across contiguous functions and a better quality of communication.

Co-location can be temporary and timed to coincide with periods when intense communication is needed. BMW has a prototype factory. It is used when introducing a 300 Series new model. All groups responsible for the re-design efforts move into the factory. The groups communicate as the design process proceeds from concept to drawings to models to full-scale clay models to a driveable prototype. The groups are product designers, manufacturing process designers, purchasing negotiators, designers of training programs, marketing product managers, and financial analysts. These groups co-locate during the communication-intense design/redesign process. When the first 250 cars of the new model are built and tested, the groups disband and return to their functional locations to interact with fellow professionals. The groups that will design the new 500 Series move into the prototype factory in their place.

In summary, co-location can be used to increase the quantity and quality of cross-departmental communication. Proximity is a powerful shaper of relationships. And when units are located next to one another, work-related relationships are created naturally and voluntarily. With some analysis of work flows, organization designers can increase the likelihood of the establishment of cross-departmental networks.

The preceding discussion concerns mostly cross-functional coordination in a business unit. The same discussion would apply to shared technologies across businesses in a corporation. Technologists from a core technology can be co-located even though some of them belong to other business units. The use of co-location, except on a temporary basis, does not apply to international lateral coordination.

3. Information Technology Networks. One of the most powerful current and future shapers of informal networks is the new information technology. While many of us have heard amazing predictions for years (Simon, 1960), much of what is possible is actually happening today. In addition, the projected improvements in hardware and software make multimedia workstations an economic reality. Organizations that capitalize on this technology first, and translate information technology networks into interpersonal networks, will gain an advantage.

Hardware continues its relentless increase in capacity and decrease in size and weight. The raw capacity to compute, store, and transmit information doubles every one to three years, depending on the technology. As a result, the integration of text, video, and audio applications becomes more feasible. Miniaturization continues to shrink the size of the devices that we use to compute and communicate. Software advances facilitate user interface. Combined, these advances create powerful, convenient, and easy-to-use communication devices for all employees.

The consequence of this technology is that every person in the organization may communicate with every other person at his or her own discretion. The technology has the potential to remove significant barriers to communication. Barriers of time and space can be overcome, as well as organizational barriers of hierarchy and department. The organization becomes opened up to virtually limitless communication. It is the role of organization designers to shape relationships and networks that may result from the technology.

Informal networks or communities of interest will spring up naturally, as anyone familiar with electronic mail can attest. It is very easy for someone to broadcast, "Anyone interested in XXX, please contact sender. Next steps will follow." When people respond, a network is born. These informal networks may not facilitate organizational goals. In order to increase the likelihood of networks supporting organizational goals, organization designers can create data bases and form networks. For example, an accessible personnel data base is a great aid to networking and relationship formation. The data base contains lists of all personnel, along with their past responsibilities, current responsibilities, and interests and skills. Then, someone working on, say, a neural net program may access all other people having neural net skills and/or interests. The network is still formed at the discretion of the individual. The data base makes the contacts easier to establish and use. The contacts can be used for answering questions, sharing ideas, and establishing face-to-face meetings.

Organization designers can take a more active role and create the opportunity for networks to form. For example, an electronic mail account may be created for all managers in sales, marketing, distribution, and finance whose responsibilities include WalMart. Sales could gather information from all these sources prior to suggesting a change or making a proposal to WalMart. Similarly, all engineers working on design projects where Sony is the partner could share an account. Data bases on WalMart and Sony could be made available and updated. The information network can be simple or complex, depending on the priority of the issue. Virtually any issue could be addressed in this way. All managers whose responsibilities include a common product, project, customer, vendor, competitor, technology, union, or whatever could be electronically linked. The membership for these computer conferences can also be controlled, with participants usually selected more for their expertise and knowledge than for their rank in the hierarchy.

Software is appearing that facilitates the formation of informal networks (*Fortune,* March 23, 1992, p. 93). Lotus has produced NOTES software, which creates multiple bulletin boards that can be queried and used. Price Waterhouse has 9000 employees hooked up via NOTES. Even more powerful is Groupware, developed at the University of Arizona and sold in various versions by IBM and NCR (Johansen, 1988). Video versions are currently under design. People interact using Groupware by typing into the system. All people who are interacting type at one time and their ideas appear anonymously on everyone's screen. The process is faster and more effective than verbal meetings. People can type simultaneously but not talk simultaneously. People read faster than they listen. In meetings individuals dominate; with Groupware everyone inputs equally and anonymously. Proponents see Groupware as the non-discriminatory democratization of data. The ideas and information stand alone and independent of the age, gender, ethnic group, or hierarchical level of their originators. The software has the potential of eliminating classical and heretofore enduring barriers to communication.

The new technologies will allow groups to form electronically. Resources can be tapped independently of their physical location. Savage and Digital Equipment Corporation refer to these groups as virtual (almost) teams (Savage, 1992). Anywhere a skill resides in an organization, it can be linked to others. Truly location-free organization will be an enormously useful tool for international coordination.

As stated, hardware and software advances are creating information networks that connect everyone in rapid, efficient, and easy-to-use communication systems. Already the promise of the technology is being demonstrated. In order to capitalize on the information technology network, organizations need to create informal personal networks to complement them.

The technology connects everyone. But to be effective, connection must lead to communication. For communication to occur, the participants must share a common language and understanding. Companies must develop and value cross-cultural sensitivities to communicate with various subcultures. Rotation policies destroy stereotypes and create people who learn jargon and languages. The company reward system needs to recognize and value these skills.

Thus information technology presents a new opportunity to create informal networks. The hardware and software are making it easier for ordinary people to communicate using the technology. The new technology has great potential for reducing powerful barriers to communication. When combined with personal networks, information technology networks will be an enhancer of the lateral organization.

4. Interdepartmental Events. The variety of interdepartmental events that can be used for creating relationships is virtually limitless. The most common one is training. Companies will send groups of 25 managers to a two-week session on some topic. At the end of two weeks, the company has 25 people trained on the topic. But the company also discovers that they have 25 people who know each other, and some who will continue their contact after the two weeks are over. Like rotation programs, the relationship-building that accompanies training was initially seen as a side benefit. Today, training departments justify their budgets based on *both* training and relationship-building. The next step is to select people whose work interacts and among whom communication is required. The session becomes one of both training and team-building around an interface. The people and the organizations both benefit.

Similar benefits can be derived from the many quarterly and annual meetings at which managers from around the world gather to discuss business results. Often these meetings are partly justified because of the networks created at breaks, dinner, or in the hospitality suite. Again, a little design of the seating arrangements, agenda items, and informal time can increase the likelihood that key relationships are formed.

One general manager gathers his management team from around the world for quarterly, two-day meetings. All managers gather for dinner on the Tuesday night before the two-day session. The dinner is informal, and the meeting that follows is under the control of the managers. The general manager in charge does not attend. The managers from the business units have found this evening to be so successful that they are using it with their own staffs.

In summary, the potential exists to create informal networks by adding some design thinking to activities that the organization undertakes anyway. Some ingenuity applied to interdepartmental experiences, training sessions, and other events can create informal relationships that can be drawn upon when using the lateral organization. Other policies can also be used to directly create these relationships by making structural changes. These changes are described in the next section.

Mirror-Image Departments

Vast numbers of interfaces are a major barrier to coordinating workflows. The mirror-image structure reduces the number of interfaces, thus facilitating the usefulness of the informal organization across the company.

The functional organizations making up a business unit would particularly benefit from this structural change. For example, a typical consumer goods manufacturing division has a sales force that is organized by geography and major accounts. Marketing is organized by brands, manufacturing by plant site and process, engineering by product and technology, and purchasing by commodity and vendor. If an engineer has an idea for a new product or a change to an existing product, he or she must communicate and convince 20 other departments. Outside of engineering, there are 4 groups in purchasing, 6 in manufacturing, 4 in marketing, and 6 in sales, all of whom are affected by the change. The frustration of communicating to 20 groups is exceeded only by the fact that a small minority can stall or block an idea altogether. The proposal can be escalated to the divisional management teams, but only if the company has the luxury of time and only on one or a few products. When working on multiple product lines under time compression, escalation is possible for only a few high-priority ideas.

Some organizations are speeding decisions by creating lower-level equivalents of the division staff for each product or customer segment. These organizations are aligning functional structures so that each function presents a single interface to the other functions. In Fig. 3.2, an airframe manufacturer has organized each function by major section of the aircraft. Each function has a wing department and so on. There is the equivalent of a division staff for the wing, the fuselage, and the avionics.

There is a clear line of sight through the division for the wing. An engineer making a change will have 5 or 6 units, not 20, with which to negotiate. Each of the 5 or 6 functional managers will be responsible for the wing. All of the members of the network have the information and authority to decide for their section. The communications will be faster and probably more effective as a result. Relationships among the people can more easily be created and maintained. Each functional organization is a mirror image of the others. The collection of all functional units on the wing becomes the equivalent of a general manager for the wing.

The good news is that the speed of communication, decision-making, and action will be faster. The bad news is that the function may lose specialization or may duplicate people for each

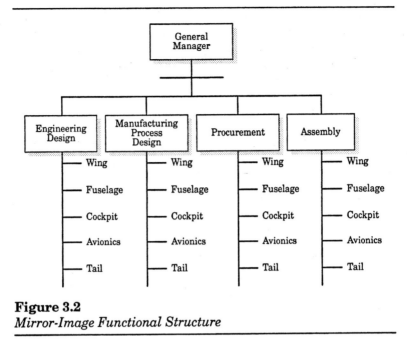

Figure 3.2
Mirror-Image Functional Structure

product section. Some companies will choose speed over cost of duplication to get faster time-to-market. Others will create a matrix within the function. Quality will organize by major section of the aircraft, but also by support units for specialists in statistics and nondestructive testing. Another unit using expensive test equipment will centralize and share the equipment across all aircraft section units. The complexity will be managed within rather than between the functions.

Thus, structural changes can facilitate the formation of relationships by creating mirror-image functions or units to be coordinated. Similar structures can be created to coordinate businesses across countries. The change minimizes interfaces and the number of people a person needs to know and work with. Managers can know each other better and share a common perspective and responsibility. The likelihood of voluntary cooperation will increase.

Consistent Reward and Measurement Systems

One of the keys to aligning the interests of the members of the informal organization with those of the company is the reward and measurement system. To the degree that clear, acceptable, and understandable measures can be articulated, the power of the informal networks can be channeled toward company goals and performance. Considerable progress has been made recently toward removing inter-unit barriers and aligning interests.

Different and incompatible goals have always been a barrier to cooperation across units. Usually the customer's priorities are different from those of unit's hierarchical boss. Before, the boss's priorities became the unit's priorities. The company quality programs have been a major factor in reducing the incompatibility between goals. Each unit now surveys its customers to see what is required of them, and differences are being resolved by the management teams. Most companies are now setting goals that are consistent across units and are less of a barrier to cooperation. The most powerful force, however, has been the articulation of a single overarching goal that can guide all of the units that need to communicate and cooperate. Some companies, like Procter & Gamble, have formed a total supply function that combines engineering, purchasing, manufacturing, and distribution in a single unit. They have been measured by a Total Delivered Cost metric. The metric allows trade-offs between different costs incurred by the different functions. Total delivered cost to the customer is the conflict resolver. It is also the basis for measuring and rewarding people in the functions.

Today, more companies are using a measure of time as the overarching goal measurement (Stalk and Hout, 1990). Cycle time, or time-to-market, is becoming a common goal shared by everyone along a work flow. People can identify with time ("time is money"), measure it, and understand it. Hewlett-Packard uses a measure of Break Even Time (BET). It measures time from the start of a new product program to the time when the product revenue matches costs invested in the product. It measures not just speed but quality. They do not want to be fast to market and then repair the product in the field.

These overarching goals serve as criteria for cross-unit decision making and measures of performance for rewarding accomplishment. They align goals across units and give them unity of purpose. The goals also serve to align the interests of informal groups with those of the organization.

Investment banks are an instructive example. They require spontaneous cooperation from specialists in various departments to complete a deal rapidly. Yet they grant very large individual bonuses. Management has evolved a subjective assessment process that consumes an enormous amount of management's time. Most banks have given up attempting to assign revenues to individuals and departments. Revenue and fee splitting always lead to dysfunctional conflicts and arguments. Instead, revenue goes to the bank as a whole. Individuals are evaluated by management thoughout the year and at the completion of every deal. Management assesses people's contributions based on conversations with customers, peers, other departments, and the individuals themselves. The goal is to evaluate people flexibly on their contribution to total revenue. Up to 25 percent of management's time is invested in clarifying criteria and assessing a person's total contributions to teams completing transactions. The measures are fuzzy, but the process eliminates dysfunctions and encourages cooperation among specialists.

The other purpose of the measurements is to promote cooperation. Cooperation, or integration, is the ultimate purpose of the lateral organization. As shown in Fig. 3.3, the practices described in this chapter establish connections among people.

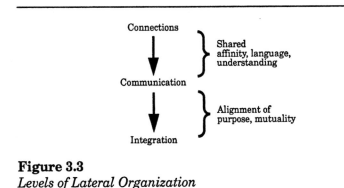

Figure 3.3
Levels of Lateral Organization

Common locations and personal-computer networks connect people. When there is some affinity for one another and shared language and understanding, connection leads to communication. The sharing of information and ideas within the informal network can lead to substantial payoffs. By itself, communication may justify the cost of the practices needed to create the network. But the real payoff, via improved communication, is the achievement of integration and coordination across organizational units. The voluntary and spontaneous integration will occur if goals are aligned across units and payoffs are mutual; that is, it takes an organization that is designed to act spontaneously and voluntarily. This design combines the various practices described in this section. Relationships are created through events and rotational experiences. Relationships are used for communication through co-location and information technology. Communication is then used to integrate action, to achieve aligned goals. The result is the lateral organization, which is a lasting competitive advantage.

An Example—Cathay Pacific

Cathay Pacific is the airline of Hong Kong. It has offices throughout the world and routes that connect them. These far-flung activities are integrated with an effective lateral organization.

Central to the functioning of the lateral organization is the overarching goal of *route profitability*. What is important is to make routes profitable, not individual countries. For example, a route may run from Seoul to Hong Kong to Bangkok to Bahrain to London Heathrow. The airline does not want to book a piece of business from Seoul to Bangkok if its precludes booking a more profitable piece of business from Hong Kong to London. On the other hand, if it is a good Seoul customer and another booking can be made from Bangkok to London, priority should go to the Seoul customer. All of this discussion takes place among managers in the countries and managers of routes. These discussions take place hundreds of times each day under time pressure. Once the plane takes off, the opportunity is lost. So Cathay Pacific is a very communication-intense organization constantly meeting deadlines around the world. The decisions are guided by route-profitability measures.

The system could not be managed without a worldwide reservation system. Therefore, all offices are connected with terminals and PCs in a worldwide telecom network. The network maintains global seat and cargo inventories around which the negotiations take place. Telephone and, increasingly, video contacts become the vehicles for discussions. But it is the marriage of the worldwide information technology network and the informal network that makes Cathay Pacific effective.

The informal network begins with the selection process. Recruits are selected by John Swires, whose family has run trading and shipping businesses out of Hong Kong for generations. Each year he selects five or six graduates from Oxford who he believes will thrive in the Far East. These people are low-ego, self-effacing personalities who can understand the Oriental practice of "saving face." He dines with them and refuses to hire anyone with whom he cannot enjoy a good meal. The result is a group of managers from various ethnic groups who speak English, share a common background, and develop a great deal of affinity. The managers rotate among countries, functions, routes, and headquarters. Recently the author met the vice president of personnel for Japan. Previously he ran operations in Korea. He is an Australian who speaks Japanese and Korean. There are quarterly meetings in Hong Kong for the top managers of countries, routes, and functions. Members of the top 250 managers participate in management-development programs conducted for the company by INSEAD. Swires likes INSEAD because it is located in Fountainbleu, France. There is nothing to do in Fountainbleu, and it is too far from Paris to travel there and back in an evening. The managers who participate in the program, 25 at a time, have nothing to do but work together on business cases for three weeks. At the completion of the course, Cathay Pacific has 25 trained managers and 25 people who know each other very well. Each class recreates the company in microcosm. The members represent the various countries, routes, and functions. Upon completion of the course, they will return to positions around the world to negotiate for route profitability.

In summary, Cathay Pacific has blended the practices of selection, rotation, and training not only to develop people but to create an informal network. This network is tied together by a worldwide telecommunications network showing seat and cargo inventories. These inventories are constantly changed, updated, and negotiated in order to maximize route profitability. Collectively these policies created by John Swires compose the lateral organization of Cathay Pacific.

4

Formal Lateral Groups

The lateral organization described in the last chapter was the voluntary organization. It arises spontaneously out of the day-to-day transactions across the units of the organization's structure. As such, it is tantamount to organizing from the bottom up. Top management, however, could influence the formation of the voluntary organization by such human resource policies as rotational careers and supporting reward systems. This chapter describes the formal lateral organization, which is more of a top-down design. Rather than being a substitute for the voluntary organization, however, the formal organization builds on the same foundation that is needed for the former. The organization is more formal because top management takes a more active role in its creation and maintenance.

Formality

The lateral organization becomes more formal as management exerts a greater role in shaping it. There are a number of reasons for management to take a more active role. The first occurs when lateral coordination is required for an issue and the voluntary organization does not emerge to manage it. Management must then create cross-departmental groups to coordinate the solution to the issue. Or management may become aware of an issue first. The hierarchical division of labor places management in a position to take a longer-term and more external view than lower-level managers. That vantage point may lead to earlier recognition of the need to act.

The top-down approach is also needed to augment and overcome the weaknesses of the bottom-up approach. The power of the voluntary organization is its "grass-roots" responsiveness, its access to local data, and the involvement of those who are closest to and most knowledgeable about the work. At the same time, it is local and provincial, and the participants may not have access to external data and may lack a global perspective. For example, a group may form to deal with a cross-border issue in Europe. Management may see the issue as having global significance rather than just a regional European impact. Management may want to redefine the mission and to increase or change the membership of the group involved. Management may want to assign a manager who would develop and profit from the experience. The group may need more- or less-experienced people. The solution may require resources beyond the authority of those currently involved. Thus management, from its more global perspective, may shape the effort to be more compatible with other efforts, resources, and overall strategy.

Management must also set priorities on which kinds of lateral organization to use. In today's flat structures, there is a limited amount of managerial time available for lateral organizational efforts. There is also a tendency to use a team or a task force on every issue. Within a business unit there are calls for teams for products, teams for customers, teams for improvements, teams for processes, teams for partners, and any other kind of team. Where should the organization be using its talent? Management's task is to set strategy and focus the organization in its use of its talents. By creating and defining the lateral organization's mission and charter, management will set priorities for the efforts of the managers. So by creating cross-unit efforts, by augmenting the voluntary efforts, and by setting priorities among competing efforts, management will formalize parts of the lateral organization.

Formal Groups

The need for the creation of formal groups was partly addressed in the previous section. In addition, strategies of diversity, global integration, and value added will require more lateral coordination in the form of more decisions. Additional general management decision-making is needed for these strategies.

And for companies with large numbers of people, large numbers of organizational units, and wide geographic spread, the voluntary organization will need to be supplemented.

The formal groups that supplement the voluntary organization go by many names, such as task forces, teams, boards, councils, and committees. There does not seem to be any standard definition across industries for these formal groups. However, the terms "teams" and "teamwork" are the ones most often used to describe the use of groups in decision-making. In all cases, they are cross-departmental groups. Recall that the objective is to recreate the organization in microcosm for the issue at hand; that is, all units that have a stake in the issue need to be represented in the group. If a large number of units are affected by an issue, the group will involve managers at a high hierarchical level. If few units are involved, the group would consist of lower-level managers. In each case the intent is to create the equivalent of a general manager for the issue. Normally a general manager would have seen that the issue was resolved. But given the number of decisions required by the strategy, additional general management decision capacity is needed. The additional capacity is provided by the cross-departmental group.

The Design of Groups

There is currently a great deal of writing about using teams (Cohen, 1993; Smith and Katzenbach, 1992). There has also been a good deal of writing about team building and making teams effective (Dyer, 1988). In an earlier book, the author discussed some design issues in creating teams (Galbraith, 1973). These topics are still valid and will not be treated extensively here. Instead, a brief summary of the design issues will be given and then they will be discussed in the context of the lateral coordination needs of business units, international organization, and the corporation.

All groups, no matter what type, have some design choices in common. These are briefly presented as follows.

1. Basis. The design of groups requires the same balancing of pros and cons as that of the choice of organization structure (Tushman and Nadler, 1988). Groups can be created around the same dimensions as the hierarchy. If the hierarchy is geographic, then teams can be functional-, business-, supplier-, or customer-based, to name some of the choices. The strategy for the organization is the guide to the choice of dimensions of lateral coordination.

2. Charter. The groups need to have their scope and authority defined. They have to be compatible with the hierarchical structure and to augment it. Which decisions, issues, and resource levels the group can commit should be defined to allow clarity of purpose, and avoid conflict and overlap with other efforts.

3. Staffing. The choice of participants in a group is central to its effective functioning. Besides choosing a representative from each affected unit, the people should come from a level and position within the unit so that they possess the information relevant to the issue. In addition, they need to have sufficient authority so that they can commit their unit. Decision making requires that these people possess both the information and the authority. Then the group can collectively decide on an action.

4. Conflict. The group needs an approach to managing the inevitable differences of point of view that arise. Each participant comes to the group seeing a different part of the elephant, so to speak. The group needs to develop its own process for resolving differences and focusing on problems and results. Some of the many team-building approaches will be useful for creating a process for managing conflict.

5. Rewards. Participants will have little energy with which to confront conflict and problem solve if they perceive little reward resulting from their efforts (Lawler, 1990). Like the reward-system ideas discussed in the previous chapter, rewards around group outcomes and performance should be counted in the total evaluation of people participating on cross-unit teams.

6. Leader Role. An issue requiring more discussion is whether the group needs a leader and, if so, from what unit the person should come. For some groups with a reasonable number of members and some self-management experience, a designated leader may not be required. Instead, a different lead role will emerge depending on the issue at hand and who in the group is most competent to handle it.

Most organizations, however, designate a leader to plan the agenda, convene the group, lead discussions, and communicate to others about the group's work. This minimal role can be expanded into a full-time integrator. (This role is discussed in Chapter 5.) There are several practices that can be used before going to a full-time integrator. One is to use a leader from the unit most affected by the group's work. Or management can select a leader from the dominant unit. Boeing design teams are led by the project engineers. Brand teams at Procter & Gamble are led by brand managers from advertising. Their work most closely resembles the leadership role.

Another model is rotating the leadership. Dow-Corning rotates the leader role in new product groups as the product progresses from design to implementation. In the early phases, when R&D is most active, the leader comes from R&D. When the product moves into the factory, the leader comes from manufacturing. When the product moves into the marketplace, the leader comes from sales and marketing. During all phases, the group is multifunctional, and members stay with the group throughout. Only the leader role rotates. The group gets the effect of a general management leader role over this period, but it gets it sequentially, through hand-offs from leader to leader.

For lateral groups that are more strategically important and more difficult to manage, however, a full-time and neutral leader role is necessary. This leader role is the integrator role, which will be described in Chapter 5.

Thus, the design of lateral groups involves using all the organizational dimensions described in the Star Model in Chapter 1. There are considerations of structure, staffing, rewards, and leadership for all types of teams. The choice criteria are supplied by the strategy. The policies are chosen in order to provide alignment.

Cross-Functional Groups

Companies are most experienced in using the lateral organization across functions. Aerospace was an early example. Aerospace companies had to coordinate multiple projects for different customers (for example, the Air Force, the Navy, and NASA). By forming cross-functional project teams they could coordinate the work from design to delivery and bring additional general management decision-making to the organization. A similar capability was created for manufacturing businesses with several product lines, or service businesses with several market segments. Consumer banking businesses formed groups for high-networth customers, the elderly, small businesses, and the mass market. In each case, cross-functional groups were used to manage diversity and provide additional general management decision-making.

In the 1980s, cross-functional coordination requirements increased. First, the Total Quality movement gained speed, and it was followed by Time Based Competition initiatives described in Chapter 2. Then there were all the "design for _____" issues, such as "design for quality," and "design for manufacturability." In the 1990s the requirements will be "design for re-use" and "re-manufacturing." Most countries are demanding that products be recycled.

All of the "design for _____" efforts require the early integration of other functions into the design process with the product design engineers. As a result, all manufacturing companies are now using concurrent design or simultaneous engineering processes; that is, the design of manufacturing processes, training programs, vendor selection, and whatever else is necessary, all occur simultaneously with the design of the product. These initiatives greatly increase the interdependence among functions; these functions all contribute to new product development. All of these processes require more coordination and decision-making across the functions. Cross-functional groups for new products have been a dominant type of formal group.

The design of cross-functional groups tries to give the group a total end-to-end responsibility across all functions. Sometimes the end-to-end responsibility takes place around a product line for a new product design. Other times it takes place around the work flow for product lines, or what are called core processes (Kaplan and Murdock, 1991; Ostroff and Smith, 1992). The new product development process is one of the core processes. Another is the order-generation and fulfillment process for existing products. The process consists of the generation of an order by sales. The order then sequentially involves finance in order processing and credit checking, product engineering for any design modifications, purchasing for new material, component manufacturing, assembly, logistics and delivery, and, finally, finance again for invoicing and collection. In order for the process to work flawlessly and rapidly, a cross-functional group will be dedicated to managing the total work flow. There may be several teams for different products with different flow characteristics.

The new information technology makes time compression and the process orientation possible. However, the cross-functional management systems for quick reaction usually have to be completely redesigned to support cross-functional decisions. These redesign efforts are popularly called re-engineering (Hammer, 1990; Heygate and Breback, 1991). These new systems are cross-functional and process oriented.

Some people even believe the trend is toward process organization. Hewlett-Packard is investigating a dual organization of functions and processes. The R&D manager will be responsible for the R&D function and new product development processes. All new-product cross-functional teams will report to the R&D manager. The manufacturing manager will be responsible for the manufacturing function and the order-fulfillment process. Cross-functional work-flow groups will also report to the manufacturing manager. The managers reporting to the general manager for a business will be responsible for a function and a set of cross-functional teams responsible for core process design and operation.

Boeing is facing challenges in all these areas on its 777 project. It is using over 240 cross-functional groups to manage these challenges. It is trying to reduce the eight-year product-development cycle down to around five years. It is also trying to design for easier manufacturing, quality, and ease of repair. At the same time, it is trying to be responsive to its customers, the world's airlines, each of which wants something unique on its airplanes.

The organization structure for the program is the basic functional organization. The lateral organization is a hierarchy of groups and a cross-linkage of multidimensional groups. Some of the groups are design/build teams consisting of all the functions that design and manufacture the airplane. These teams are formed around sections of the aircraft, as shown in Fig. 3.2. The major sections are further subdivided into work-package teams in which the actual engineering and manufacturing

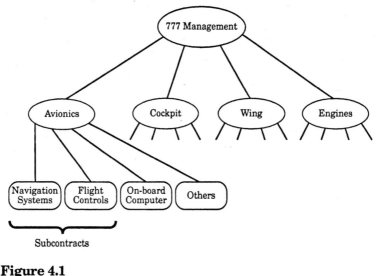

Figure 4.1
The 777 Design / Build Hierarchy

design work takes place. Many of the packages are subcontracted to the first-tier vendors. Figure 4.1 shows the design/build hierarchy. Each circle represents a cross-functional team.

Hierarchy of Design/Build Teams

Vendors participate in teams like Avionics, where significant portions are subcontracted. Vendors use Boeing's CAD/CAM system and are linked electronically into the design process. Indeed, it is the CAD system that integrates much of the interdependence between design/build teams internal and external to Boeing.

Another set of teams has been created for major customer segments. For customers who commit early to a new program and order a significant number of aircraft, a cross-functional team is created to work with them. Customers all desire unique features. Some features—such as interior colors and design—are of minor consequence to the design of the airplane. But Lufthansa may want the design in metric units and the hydraulic systems to use German pump vendors. Japanese

Airlines (JAL) may want food-preparation galleys to be smaller and located differently than United Airlines (UA). Shifting galleys changes the center of gravity of the airplane and requires re-stressing the floors. These changes can cause major redesign efforts. The cross-functional teams must formulate the changes, determine their costs and consequences, and negotiate a price with the customer.

The two types of teams need to be linked. They need to resolve the never-ending conflicts arising from customer requests for a different design and the design/build team's interest in making the design the same. The design/build team would minimize its costs, complexity, and time-to-market if every customer bought the same cockpit design. However, each airline's pilots and training programs prefer and use different systems. The customer team negotiates between the customer representatives and the design/build team. The interlinkage of the two types of teams is shown in Table 4.1. Some sections of the airplane, like the wings, require little or no customer modification. Others, like the cockpit, require substantial negotiation. For these sections there are engineering representatives that are members of both teams. These people play key linking roles between customer teams and design/build teams.

The top team has the responsibility to resolve conflicts that cannot be handled at lower levels. This team, shown in Fig. 4.2, approves the preliminary design, sets parameters for the overall plan, and creates criteria for team decision-making. They will track the overall weight of the plane, its estimated cost, and the completion date. Each team is given budgets for weight, cost, and milestones. If a team can reduce weight by using a more expensive material, they will be guided by the criterion of dollars per pound set by management. If the suggestion is within the criterion, the team can make the decision and proceed. If weight, cost, or time is to be increased, the team is given other parameters for choosing and resolving conflicts. If parameters are exceeded, the issue is raised to the next-level team for resolution.

The top team also has links to other parts of the group. The purchasing function buys aluminum, semiconductors, and wiring for all Boeing aircraft (747, 767, 757). United Airlines buys all types of airplanes. They want common baggage-handling systems across all aircraft. Thus there are numerous

Table 4.1
Interlinked Teams

	United Airlines	Singapore Airlines	Jal	European Airlines	Asian Airlines	Small Airlines
Avionics	X		X	X		
Cockpit	X	X	X	X	X	
Fuselage	X	X	X	X	X	X
Tail						
Wing						
Engines	X			X		
. . .						

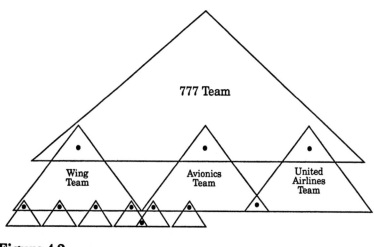

Figure 4.2
Hierarchy and Interlinkages of Teams

linkages across airplane programs that are handled at various levels by the functions, but coordinated by the top team.

The top team, therefore, is the designer of the system of groups. They set the strategy for the airplane, approve the plan, create criteria for decentralized decision-making within and among teams, provide interlinkages within the program and among programs, and resolve major issues that exceed the criteria given to the teams. They play a key role in orchestrating the entire effort.

Boeing has thus created a multidimensional organization for the 777 program. The hierarchical structure is functional. The engineering function, in particular, is staffed with specialists in aerodynamics, carbon fiber structures, and electrohydraulics. These specialists move from one airplane program to another as new designs are undertaken and are grouped into design/build teams around sections of the airplane. Others are grouped into customer teams. Interlinkages between groups and the top team integrate the functional, customer, and product dimensions of the organization. They have both a structural and a group hierarchy.

In summary, lateral groups across functions can vary from being rather simple to very complex. Diversity of products and markets and time compression are the primary strategic factors that necessitate organizational complexity. A single-product business with normal time demands, like some breweries, can be functional with only a voluntary lateral organization. Another single-product business under time pressure can be functional with process teams for new products, and order management for existing products. An aerospace firm or a bank with multiple projects or multiple market segments will have a functional structure with project teams or segment teams. These are two-dimensional businesses. And, finally, Boeing has a structure with three dimensions. They have a functional structure, but they augment it with design/build product teams and customer teams. Boeing is facing demanding customers, time compression, and a business strategy of multiple sources of diversity. Its groups are formal, multidimensional, and hierarchical.

International Groups

The application of the lateral organization to international business is a topic of increasing interest. Companies are experiencing the twin demands from strategies for global integration and global dispersion. Together they demand too much coordination across countries to use only the organization's hierarchy. In addition, the voluntary organization is less likely to emerge across the simultaneous hierarchic, geographic, and language boundaries. Managements are therefore implementing formal groups, while at the same time encouraging the voluntary organization. As a result, these formal groups must keep the natural boundaries from becoming barriers.

In some ways, the lateral organization across countries is similar to the one described across functions. The purpose is to create a general manager equivalent for cross-country issues. For example, Honeywell was organized by geographic profit centers around the world. When they experienced an increased need for global integration because of investments in R&D, they created global strategy teams for their Residential Controls, Commercial Controls, and Industrial Controls businesses. The person responsible for the business in major countries like the United States, United Kingdom, France, Germany, and Japan, and representatives from some smaller countries, formed the strategy teams. The teams then formulated a global strategy for the business. In particular, they were interested in coordinating R&D investments and microprocessor development. The teams met quarterly, communicated frequently, and once a year reviewed their strategy at the headquarters in Minneapolis. When approved, the strategy set guidelines for the preparation of yearly budgets and profit commitments of country managers for the following year. This process integrated the business and country goals for the fiscal year. Thus, as companies with geographic organization structures experienced the need to coordinate businesses with increasing R&D investments, they formed worldwide business teams with the participation of the large-country business managers and representatives for the smaller countries. These teams were to formulate global strategy, share investments in R&D, and coordinate new product development to the extent that it was needed.

Eaton Corporation, in contrast to Honeywell, was organized around businesses that had worldwide responsibilities. In major countries where it was valuable to speak with one voice, Eaton formed country councils. The councils consisted of the managers who were responsible for the businesses in the country. The manager with the largest business became the council leader. The council would formulate a company position on legislative issues, coordinate recruiting programs, and decide on the company stance in union negotiations. With the formation of a single market in Europe, the largest businesses in the large countries have formed a regional council. Country councils are still used in the rest of the world. Thus, formal business groups are formed to coordinate across geographic profit centers, and formal country and regional groups are formed to coordinate across global business profit centers.

The design of these international structures and groups is the easy part. Getting the groups and managers to function effectively is another issue. Most companies are finding that their ability to formulate global strategies and design global organizational structures and processes far exceeds the ability of their managers to function effectively within those structures. The reasons for the difficulty are obvious. Managers do not yet have the skills to manage the ethnic and cultural diversity, the multiple languages, and the variety of business practices that are experienced in international business. Most companies lack the human resources who know how to think, act, lead, and participate in a global business context. Until more managers are developed, the lateral organization will be underdeveloped.

Companies have tried some practices to overcome the difficulties. The first practice tried by all newcomers to international business is to use expatriates. They create a few managers who can function in other countries, place them in positions of responsibility, and link them with the national headquarters through global business teams. These cosmopolitans help bridge the cultural gap between the headquarters and the foreign subsidiary. Expatriates improve global coordination but also cause problems. The local, native managers in foreign subsidiaries can become resentful of imported expatriates and feel like second-class citizens. The company finds it difficult to attract and hold competent locals. In addition, the expatriates are not integrated into local markets and business communities. They are less effective business managers as a result.

Eventually, the company trains and develops confidence in locals to run the subsidiaries. But they still need to integrate subsidiaries if their business requires global integration. Finally, companies develop human resource practices to create managers to participate in the international lateral organization. People are hired who will function effectively in other countries. They are trained in cross-cultural differences and international team building. After learning the corporate ways of doing business, the managers move to an assignment outside their country of nationality. As they rotate to other assignments, those who are successful stay on the international track. Those who use their network successfully in the voluntary organization will be assigned to international business teams. Those who are successful in international teams will become global business managers. In this way, the company builds an international lateral organization and internationally competent managers simultaneously, by starting with the human resources practices (Evans, Laurent, and Doz, 1990). These practices build relationships which form the voluntary organization. The formal lateral organization is then built upon the foundation of the informal organization.

Another development that will facilitate international groups is the advent of global telecommunications networks. Already, computer companies like DEC and H-P use their own products to coordinate worldwide product-development efforts. While some face-to-face sessions are still needed, day-to-day communications take place via electronic networks, computer conferencing, and video conferences. Electronically mediated communication, however, will still require language skills and sensitivities to ethnic diversity.

In summary, the international use of the lateral organization rests on the development of international human resource practices. These practices equip managers who are so inclined with skills to think, act, and lead in international contexts (Pucik, Tichy, and Barnett, 1992). The process of creating these skills also generates networks for these managers which can be used for lateral coordination. These personal networks will be greatly enhanced with the development of electronic networks. Initially the lateral coordination will be implemented through the voluntary organization. The human resource practices will lay the foundation for more formal coordination mechanisms, which will be required by global integration strategies.

Corporate Lateral Organization

The coordination of activities across business units is probably the least developed of the three capabilities. (Perhaps for Japanese companies it is the international activities that are the least developed.) The disappearance of the corporate staffs and the insistence on value being added to businesses due to corporate membership are requiring more lateral coordination. The bottlenecks to cross-unit coordination in the corporate case are inertia due to past practices and lack of corporate strategy.

The practice of excessive decentralization to business units retards cross-business cooperation (Porter, 1985, Chapter 11). Business-unit managers jealously guard their autonomy from interference from elsewhere in the corporation. Business-unit measurement and reward practices reinforce this attitude. But even in corporations with a cooperative climate, asymmetric payoffs retard coordination. Accounting systems have not always been flexible in giving credit for cooperative internal ventures. Also, strong businesses are less interested in cooperating with their weaker brethren. For all these reasons, cross-business-unit cooperation in American and Western companies is weak, even in cases where it is desirable.

A second barrier to lateral coordination is a lack of lateral strategy. If the corporation does not have an agreed-upon strategy for business-unit cooperation, voluntary cooperation is less likely. Companies have developed a rigorous approach to articulating and promulgating business-unit strategies. But there are few well-articulated corporate or cross-business strategies beyond the usual vision and values. There are few articulations of how business-unit coordination that is not easily copied by competitors will lead to competitive advantage. So while international lateral coordination was limited by international human resource inadequacies, it is a lack of corporate strategy that prevents corporate lateral coordination.

The situation is changing as competition focuses on capabilities (Stalk, Evans, and Schulman, 1992; Grant, 1991) and core competencies (Prahalad and Hamel, 1990). Hamel and Prahalad have laid out a strategic architecture for identifying how core competencies relate to product markets in business units. The coordination of competencies across business units then requires the same practices described earlier. The relationship between a competency in different business units is created by rotating people across the businesses, establishing an information system and shared data base, creating a joint plan for investment and development, holding annual conferences, and similar practices. If a few business units are involved, a voluntary organization may informally coordinate activities. If the competency cuts across many businesses and different countries, a formal group may be needed to generate the plan and resource needs. These groups will be effective if the design issues are addressed as well as all the organizational dimensions in the Star Model in Chapter 1.

Chief executives, feeling the pressure to show value to financial analysts, are also becoming more active in encouraging, if not forcing, cooperation. Often the encouragement is opportunistic. An aerospace CEO saw how several business units could combine on a bid for a contract. He initiated a joint bid from the businesses to the government. They won and the defense department issued one contract instead of the two that had originally been planned. A cross-divisional team was created for managing and reviewing all the projects that comprise the total contract.

The incentive compensation for the divisional managers included joint goals for the contract. The CEO also reviews how the cooperation is proceeding. The encouragement is more sustained at General Electric, where the weak business units have either been divested or merged into strong ones. The remaining strong units are more willing to cooperate with each other under Jack Welch's "boundaryless" corporation. There is still no substitute, however, for a well-developed corporate strategy.

An area that has had some success is the functional coordination across businesses in divisionalized companies. Where the businesses are related, functional councils have moved people across the corporation, transferred the best practices, combined on training programs and software packages, and held annual conferences. Usually these activities were driven by the corporate staff. Councils for engineering, manufacturing, R&D, information technology, and sales are common. In today's environment, more is being demanded of them.

The Japanese corporations have been successful in generating cross-business-unit cooperation. NEC in particular has drawn upon its total internal capabilities while competing in diverse markets. NEC is motivated to share because it sees itself competing against much larger Western rivals. NEC competes in the semiconductor, telecommunications, and computer industries. Its structure is based on these three groups, but is further subdivided into product-line profit centers, such as switching equipment in telecommunications and personal, mainframe, and super-computers. There is considerable lateral coordination across these product lines.

The lateral coordination is driven by the corporate strategy, implemented through interdivisional committees and the Corporate Business Plan, and sustained through centralized human resource practices. NEC has an explicit Computers and Communication (C&C) strategy, which seeks to exploit the convergence of these two industries (Hamel and Prahalad, 1989). The convergence is built on the evolution of semiconductor technology. The strategic plan elaborates how technologies will lead to components, components to intermediate products, intermediate products to final products, and, finally, products into systems for end users. The strategic plan is a road map that shows how each division contributes to the development of the C&C strategy. Thus, product divisions have a dual responsibility. One is to be competitive and profitable in their product markets. The other is to contribute to the development of technologies and intermediate products used by all product divisions. The corporate strategy is explicit and shared, and it designates roles for divisions.

The tactical plans for C&C are prepared by 44 cross-divisional committees. These groups are created for developing key technologies and shared products. There are temporary groups that work on projects across divisions. These are aggregated into technology groups. The technology groups are reviewed by the top-level C&C Committee. There are also groups for manufacturing technologies and software development. Thus, the collection of groups is multidimensional and arranged into a hierarchy under the guidance of the cross-divisional C&C Committee.

These interdivisional committees prepare their portion of the business plan. The planning process is itself multidimensional. One dimension involves the profit center divisions. The other includes the cross-divisional technologies and intermediate products. Business-unit managers must agree upon their business plans and cross-division plans. (Multidimensional information systems and planning processes will be discussed in greater detail in Chapter 5.) The top-management team and the C&C Committee (there is overlap in membership) then make the final investment and profit decisions.

The cross-divisional group system is sustained by cross-divisional human resource practices. Recruiting is managed centrally, and all new hires associate with the corporation, not with a division. The managers rotate across divisions in their career progressions. There are frequent cross-division training sessions and meetings. There are many opportunities to form cross-divisional contacts, relationships, and networks.

The lesson from the NEC example is the role that top management plays in articulating a corporate strategy. It is the strategy that guides the integration efforts. The planning process and interdivisional committees can be designed based on the logic of the strategy. Without the corporate strategy, interdivisional cooperation will remain opportunistic and under-developed.

The need for these formal groups varies with the corporation's portfolio strategy. Companies with strategies of unrelated diversification will not need them. Companies with mixed strategies and some value added will use a few voluntary and formal groups. Highly related businesses will have extensive use of formal groups and probably some integrating roles. Again, different strategies require different types and amounts of lateral coordination. Thus, the same design issues exist for coordinating across business units. The lateral capability must be created separately for the corporate level. Just because a company is competent at cross-functional coordination within a business unit does not mean that it will be competent at coordinating across business units. The need for cross-business coordination is increasing. However, the lateral capability is still underdeveloped. It is retarded by a tradition of business-unit autonomy and the lack of a credible corporate strategy that is shared throughout the company.

The Role of Management

On several occasions, we have alluded to management's role in the lateral organization. In this section, that role is reviewed and explicitly identified. There are four parts to that role. The first part is the formulation of a strategy that articulates and promulgates how the cross-unit coordination will create competitive advantage. The second part is building the capability in the parts of the organization that will use lateral organization. The third part is creating the formal lateral groups if they do not arise voluntarily. And finally, there is management of the day-to-day lateral efforts.

Strategy Foundation

Management's first task is see that the basic direction is clear. This means formulating a strategy showing how lateral coordination will produce business results, which are the capabilities needed to meet competition or to achieve an advantage. It was stated that in the case of cross-business-unit coordination, the lack of a corporate strategy was a major factor in the weakness of that capability. The strategy then determines where in the organization the lateral capabilities will be needed. If management chooses a strategy of diversification into multiple, unrelated businesses, they should not bother with creating a lateral capability across businesses. If, however, management chooses to diversify by growing consumer products businesses from the chemistry of fats and oils (an original Procter & Gamble strategy), management needs to create a lateral community of interest around the chemical and consumer marketing competencies. The building of that capability can then proceed. The strategy also is the basis for generating goals that can guide decisions and trade-offs across units in the lateral organization. The strategy provides the criteria for the organization design choices.

Building Capability

Management's second role is building the lateral organizational capability. Many of the developmental actions have been described, but they need to be reinforced. They need to be reinforced by pointing out that the actions need to be undertaken and sustained over a long period of time. This building of capability proceeds by creating organizational policies shown in the Star Model, as modified in Fig. 4.3. The design process proceeds in a counterclockwise sequence.

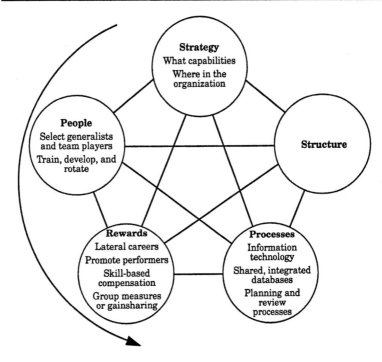

Figure 4.3
Building Lateral Capability

The type of lateral capability that is needed is built by focusing initially on the human resource practices. Management can select the generalist types who are team players, either from new graduates or existing employees. In either case, these are the people who have an affinity for lateral organizations. Those selected then receive training in cross-unit groups and rotate among groups.

The evaluation systems are then designed to reward these people for the use of their lateral skills and for results achieved by their interpersonal network. The organization can explore various pay-for-knowledge plans to reward learning different units' skills. Their success in working across units can result in a promotion to membership in a formal cross-unit group. Effective performance in a group can result in selection to chair a group. In this way, the organization creates a lateral career for generalists. Other practices and events described in Chapter 3 can be employed for people who work in the parts of the organization where lateral coordination is needed.

Management can invest in and create the information technology to support the kinds of lateral organizations that it needs. Building integrated data bases, connecting people with electronic networks, and investing in group process software are the next steps in creating lateral capability. Collectively, these steps create people practices, reward systems, and information processes (shown in Fig. 4.3) to develop a voluntary lateral organization. This lateral organization can be measured by surveys to determine its extent and quality.

There are some other skills—in addition to the capabilities already mentioned—that formal lateral groups require. These additional skills are connected with building and leading teams. Formal groups need to problem solve and resolve conflicts across organizational units. Both formal training and on-the-job training are required. For international groups these same skills are required, plus the added complexity of exercising the skills in cross-cultural settings. The cross-cultural capability is more likely to occur when foreign nationals participate in the process.

The functioning of formal groups will be facilitated by the development of information systems to support their work. The effectiveness of the cross-divisional groups at NEC and the cross-country groups at Honeywell was enhanced by their access to cross-unit information. These groups could then formulate a cross-division or country plan and determine the plan's financial consequences for the organization. The discussion and disputes can be addressed within the planning and budgeting processes. Planning and information will be elaborated in the next chapter.

Once group goals have been approved, the next step is to measure the accomplishment of these outcomes. The results can be fed back to the lateral group for their own visibility, motivation, and ongoing correction. When the performance measures are reliable, the next step is to use them to evaluate and perhaps reward the group. The group may negotiate a gainsharing agreement with management (Lawler, 1990). Future organizations may have fixed compensation based on demonstrated skills and knowledge, in addition to variable compensation based on group gainsharing agreements.

In summary, formal lateral group capability requires skills to build groups from collections of individuals, to problem solve and resolve conflicts, to resolve conflicts in multicultural settings, to provide multidimensional information systems, to achieve compatibility between vertical and lateral organizations, and to measure and reward the lateral groups accomplishments.

The Design of Formal Groups

The third management role is the design of the formal lateral group structure. Sometimes the design is straightforward. For a functional business unit with several products or several market segments, product teams and segment teams across the functions will execute the strategy. For companies operating internationally with geographical structures, teams around products or businesses will give them global integration. For companies with worldwide businesses, country or regional cross-business teams will generate some local reponsiveness to the subsidiaries and governments.

Considerably more effort must go into designing multidimensional capabilities like those described in the Boeing example. Design/build teams were used to optimize speed and cost performance. A hierarchical structure based on the structure of the airplane was devised. Customer teams were created for the customizing of the aircraft to unique demands of the airlines. Interlinkages, decision criteria for trade-offs, and a conflict-resolution process rounded out the design. Designing team structures is identical to designing organizational structures. The organization design skill is needed for the multidimensional, hierarchical, and interlinked group structures.

Managing the Lateral Process

After the lateral organization has been created, it needs to be reviewed and held accountable for its goals. Management's role is to review the groups' work for compatibility and to resolve conflicts among the multiple dimensions of the organization.

One company created a process for reviewing its functional councils, which operated across divisional profit centers. When they were started at the beginning of the year, each council would prepare a plan and determine its key results. Each council member had sub-key results which would contribute to the overall plan. This plan was reviewed, discussed, and approved by the executive committee. The committee members then factored the sub-key results into the performance reviews for all council members in their organization unit. Each council had a godfather or godmother from the executive committee to help it and the council chair. The godparent would see that the council knew the executive committee's views and, in turn, kept the executive committee informed. Occasionally the godparent would attend council meetings. The council would receive at least one other review to assess performance against key results and approve next year's proposed results. If major changes were taking place, more reviews or discussions with the council or its members would occur.

In this way, management resolved issues that needed to be raised to them and worked to see that council efforts were compatible with other company activities. The monitoring also allows management to assess the strategy, the capability-building progress, and the effectiveness of the formal group design.

Summary

This chapter has focused on the design of groups to perform lateral coordination tasks. All groups were seen to have some design issues in common. In addition, groups for coordinating across functions, countries, and business units were described, and their unique issues were identified. Finally, management's role was discussed. Management was to formulate strategy to guide the cross-unit coordination, build lateral capability over time, design the group structures, and review group performance. For some situations, additional general management decision-making will be needed. These organizations create integrating roles to help manage the voluntary lateral processes and the formal group efforts. The design of integrating roles is presented in the next chapter.

5

Integrating Roles

The previous chapters described the increasing number of business situations that require cross-unit coordination. The case was made that lateral organization was an effective means of providing this cross-unit coordination. But in order to implement the various types and amounts of lateral organization, management needs to build an organizational capability. The lateral organizational capability is the foundation for the voluntary and formal types of lateral coordination. This chapter describes the last type of formal lateral organization—the integrating role. The presence of the integrating role creates the truly flexible and multidimensional organization.

The Integrating Role

If an organization's strategy requires more general management decision-making, there is a need to invest in more management resources. This need is an extension of the argument made in earlier chapters. Diversity, time compression, and change require frequent cross-unit issues to be resolved. If members of these units can voluntarily decide on a collective response to the issue at hand, the informal organization has created the equivalent of a general manager. As more frequent and higher-priority coordination is needed across units, formal groups are created to play the general manager role with respect to the frequently occurring issues. But for some situations, a full-time, neutral manager is needed to provide the integration across organizational units.

The need for the full-time role follows from the strategies requiring more lateral coordination. More corporate value added, more global integration, more diversity, more time compression, and frequent changes in the business all require general management decision-making. The integrating role, which is a "little general manager" role, provides the capacity for more rapid and higher-quality decision-making. The cost is the investment in another management resource.

Another feature requiring the issue of the integrating role is greater differentiation (Lawrence and Lorsch, 1967); that is, strategies that lead to greater functional specialization, business diversification, and global dispersion create greater differences between organizational units. The differences are a two-edged sword. On the one hand, they lead to greater subtask performance. A pharmaceutical company employing a pharmacodynamicist will create compounds that attack diseased tissue more rapidly. But these differences make it more difficult to integrate all subtasks into the completion of the whole task. The different specialties, countries, and businesses all have their own interests, constituencies, and ways of thinking. These differences become natural barriers to integration. It is the task of the integrator to span these differences and achieve coordinated outcomes. Thus, the integrating role is to obtain better coordination, as well as more coordination.

The integrating role is more likely to provide better coordination when it is full time and neutral. When coordinating multiple constituencies, a person not from one of those constituencies may have more credibility, be seen as representing the "good of the order," and earn the trust of the participants. A full-time, neutral integrator may provide more effective leadership than a leader from one of the constituencies or a rotating leader.

More effective leadership on a set of issues may be required as multiple dimensions of a strategy become equally important. Increasing R&D investments make global integration important, but increasing protectionism also makes local citizenship important. Both the worldwide business manager and key country managers need a voice in decision-making. The addition of an integrating role makes the organizational structure more multidimensional. The company is simultaneously organized around businesses and countries. The multidimensional structure gives the organization the advantage of flexibility.

In a world of continual strategic adjustment, flexible organization is an advantage. The current organizational structure may provide focus and be aligned with today's strategy. But the current structure also constrains future strategy. The structure influences the type of information that is collected from the environment. It influences how that information is processed and how it is factored into new strategy determination. If a company has voices articulating issues for businesses, countries, markets, and functions, it is more strategically flexible and responsive. Multidimensional structure is an advantage if it is aligned with multidimensional strategy and if the differences can be managed.

In summary, several factors combine to create the need for an integrating role to supplement the lateral organization. First, the sheer volume of additional decisions to coordinate diverse units requires more general management capacity, which is delivered by the integrator. Second, greater differences among units whose work needs to be coordinated necessitates more general management time and energy to span the different boundaries. Finally, multidimensional strategies require multidimensional structures. When global business strategies give higher priority to multiple dimensions of the environment, single-dimensional hierarchies need to be supplemented by integrators who are champions of these other dimensions.

Design Issues

There are several fundamental design issues for integrating roles independently of the type. These issues all revolve around the power base from which the integrator is to influence decisions. The managers in the hierarchy have authority and control of resources. What is to be the power base of the integrator? How much power and influence does the integrator need? How does the organization capitalize on the natural contention of multiple dimensions and achieve compatibility among them?

The amount of power and influence required in the integrating role was illustrated in Table 3.1. The amount necessary will be determined by the following: the amount of value added, the amount of global integration and dispersion, and the amount of diversity and time compression. Also, the greater the differences across the units being coordinated, the greater the influence required of the integrator. So the amount of integration required by the strategy—and the difficulty in obtaining it—determine how much power and influence the integrator needs. The power base of the integrator is shaped by design decisions concerning the structure of the role, the staffing selection, the status of the role, the presence of supporting information systems, planning processes and reward systems, and the use of budget authority. Each of these features of the integrating role is described below.

Structure

The most common structure for an integrating role is to have it report to the general manager, as illustrated in Fig. 5.1. The figure shows product (although it could be project or service) managers as integrators reporting to the general manager of a business unit. Where the role reports will significantly affect its power base, its perceived influence, and its neutrality.

Another model is shown in Fig. 5.2. For businesses in which product life cycles are long, the product manager for product development reports to the R&D manager. The product manager probably chairs a cross-functional team of managers for the

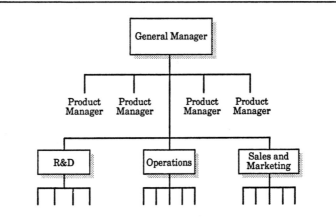

Figure 5.1
Business Unit with Product Management Integrators

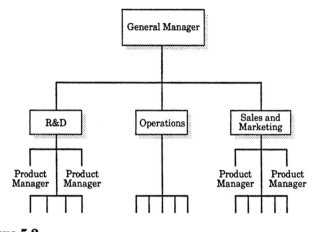

Figure 5.2
Product Management for Long Product Life Cycles

product development effort. There are also significant coordination issues within R&D that require the efforts of the integrator. After the product enters the market and there are few changes to its composition, the product manager from sales and marketing takes over and manages the day-to-day supply, advertising, and promotion. There may also be some product improvement over the years.

The sales and marketing product manager also chairs a cross-functional team for the product. The order-fulfillment process may become a responsibility for the team as well. Many consumer goods companies follow this model. The model rotates leadership across full-time integrators. Product development leadership is biased toward R&D; day-to-day product management is biased toward marketing. Over the product life cycle, a general managerial balance is achieved.

When several products, projects, and services are managed by integrators, a unit may be added to reduce the reporting span of the general manager. For example, Colgate-Palmolive introduced integrators in the 1980s to manage product categories worldwide. Colgate had operations in 50 countries and was organized by large countries and regions, as shown in Fig. 5.3.

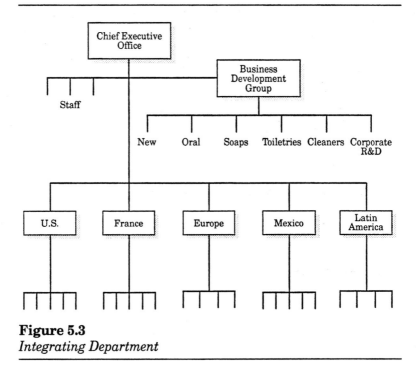

Figure 5.3
Integrating Department

A business development group was formed to coordinate worldwide R&D. Increasing investments in R&D in oral care and soaps were being made by P&G, Kao (Japan), and Unilever, all global competitors. The increased R&D investments required coordinated worldwide product development efforts. There were too many products and product categories for all of them to report to the chief executive, so the business development group was created. The manager of the business development group was to be a member of the chief executive office and was to focus on setting priorities for R&D efforts for the product categories. The coordinated R&D and product development was the role of the worldwide category manager.

Another variation is the two-hat model, which will be discussed further in the· distributed organization discussion in Chapter 6. The structure is shown in Fig. 5.4.

A director of the research function in a pharmaceutical company divided the R&D activities into functional specialties of

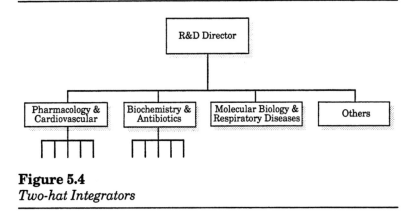

Figure 5.4
Two-hat Integrators

biochemistry, molecular biology, microbiology, statistics, and others. All of these specialties must contribute to the development of a new drug. The company had sorted its businesses into missions. One mission was to deliver cardiovascular drugs. The R&D activities were to be linked to marketing activities within the missions. Other missions were directed at respiratory diseases, infectious diseases requiring antibiotics, and other specialties. The R&D manager placed the responsibility for integration across specialties in the roles of the laboratory directors, who all directed both a specialty and a mission. Neutrality and capacity were achieved by the top team by spreading the integrating task equally across all roles.

Thus, there are several alternatives for structuring the integrating role. The usual method is to have the "little general managers" report directly to the general manager. However, considerations for the reporting span of the general manager can introduce such variations as an integrating department or a two-hat model. Products with long life cycles may profit from splitting a product management function between R&D and marketing. In all cases, the choice of structure should be guided by the power base and the neutrality of the integrator, which are necessary for the role to be effective.

Staffing

The selection of people to be integrators is probably the most important design decision in implementing integrating roles.

The reason is the scarcity of people who can successfully carry out the role. Most companies have difficulty developing or finding people for general management roles. Integrators require the same skills *plus* an ability to influence without authority. In an international context, there is still another requirement, that of influencing without authority across many cultures. Needless to say, qualified candidates for the assignment are few.

Selecting for integrators always involves compromises and settling for less than the ideal. However, some concept of the ideal is useful, particularly in designing activities and experiences to develop the people and create the capability. The wish list for the ideal integrator consists of the following: The candidate should have experience in many of the units to be integrated. Next, he or she must have the interpersonal skills to build teams and influence without authority. It helps to have low ego needs. For example, one company's training program teaches product managers that "you can either get things done *or* get credit for them, but *not both*." Integrators gain influence by always giving credit. Finally, in many situations technical competence is desirable. The integrator role gains power through neutral knowledge. The knowledge deprives members of the functions with idiosyncratic knowledge from playing expert to lay people. All of these attributes are desirable in selecting an integrator.

The choice inevitably involves a trade-off, usually between interpersonal competence and technical competence. Which is more important? Most companies have chosen integrators based on technical competence. In the author's experience, however, technical competence without interpersonal competence has always failed. Interpersonal competence appears to be critical, even in a technical organization. The integrator can usually get technical help. Selecting, developing, and training integrators to influence without authority is the key.

The best way to find these people is to grow your own supply. Creating integrators is part of creating the lateral capability. If the company selects people with varied interests and gives them inter-unit assignments, the successful ones will develop generalist skills. If these people are then given interface roles in the voluntary organization and rotated through staff roles, the successful ones will develop the skills to influence without authority. If these people are then given international assignments and roles on global strategy teams, the successful ones will develop multicultural management skills. The creation of a cadre of such people will indeed provide a competitive advantage to the company that can retain them.

Some variations in the design of the role and staffing patterns can prevent a company from settling on a candidate who is too far below the ideal. The rotating leader role is a way of sequentially getting all the needed attributes over time. Another method is to select co-managers. For example, Digital Equipment Corporation is trying to use three people to co-product manage new product development. The troika consists of a manager from engineering, one from operations, and one from sales and marketing. Kodak used two people as product manager on an early program to create electronic photography. A technical manager knew the technology and a marketing/finance manager was experienced in photography. Combined, the two had all the knowledge and experience of a general manager. In addition, they had a good personal relationship and co-managed the product development. The two or three co-managers are selected to demonstrate collectively all of the needed skills and to cooperate among themselves. Thus multiple staffing practices can sometimes serve as an alternative to making the trade-off in selecting a single integrator.

In general, going outside the company has not been effective. The generalist and technical skills may be found, and some outsiders will also know how to influence without authority. But much of what it takes to have personal influence requires local, organization-specific knowledge of a company, an appreciation of its history, and a knowledge of—and membership in—its interpersonal network. Perhaps an outsider can be paired with an accepted insider to co-manage the integrator role. Clearly, though, the best approach is create the talent along with the organizational capability.

Status

Another method of increasing an integrator's ability to influence is by upgrading or increasing the status of the role. In organizations where status and rank are important, designers should appoint high-status and/or high-ranking people. Alternatively, designers could grade the integrating role so that it merits a high rank and title. When these features of the person and the role are in place, there is an increased probability that the integrators will be able to influence people who do not work for them.

In other organizations, individuals' importance derives from the location of their office. Are they near the CEO? Are they on the top floor? On other occasions, people from particular functions or constituencies carry high status. In order to increase the status of the role, the designer should select people from these constituencies. Every organization has its way of conferring status on people and roles. The organization designer can take advantage of the status system to increase the effectiveness of the integrator role.

Information Systems

Multidimensional organizations require multidimensional information systems. Project managers in aerospace companies found they had greater influence after project information systems were developed. By having access to project costs, profits, and schedule information, project managers could negotiate with functional managers about joint goals for these measures. These companies had accounting systems which assigned costs to functions and projects.

The lack of integrated data bases and inconsistent systems across organizational units is a major barrier to integration. If product managers cannot get information for their product from all functions that work on it, they are limited in their ability to integrate. Many re-engineering projects are aimed at creating common information systems across all functions. Until everyone works from a common data base, dysfunctional conflicts can occur. Information will get brokered and shared selectively. There will be arguments about whose data are best or correct. Companies that have created common data bases available to all members of product groups find a significant increase in honesty and fewer data games. One company has adopted a slogan, "Everyone is entitled to their own opinion but not to their own data."

The informational system across countries is another impediment to global product or business management. A global product or business manager needs to see global inventories, costs, profits, and market share. However, country managers often "manage" the data and spread overheads across products to reduce questions from headquarters. The effectiveness of integrating roles will be limited until valid information can be generated. An important power base of integrating roles is knowledge and competence in their strategic dimension. It takes continuous information to sustain that level of knowledge and expert power.

Planning Processes

Another benefit of a multidimensional information system is that it will enable a multidimensional planning process. The planning process, when based on valid data, can serve as a conflict-resolving, problem-solving arena for making multidimensional trade-offs. Problem solving among line managers and integrators gives the integrators a voice in the goals of the organization; the planning process gives the integrators an arena in which to exercise influence.

The planning process is increasingly used as a method of resolving the inevitable conflicts among the different dimensions of the organization. The planning process needs to be characterized by several features in order to serve as an arena for conflict resolution. The first feature is an information system that is capable of displaying data on multiple dimensions. Usually the data are displayed on a matrix, like the one shown in Fig. 5.5, for regions and business dimensions. A matrix for functions, products, markets, core competencies, core processes, or any other dimensions could also be used.

The planning process for the time period involves the business manager and the regional manager debating and agreeing on sales, profits, and market shares for that business in that region for the time period of the plan. Invariably there are differences among the managers. The North American manager will be interested in total profit (Total A) for the region. The Business I manager may be interested in growing market share in North America and less interested in this year's profit. The Latin American manager may want more market share and growth than the business manager is willing to sponsor in the Latin American region. The business manager may be concerned about greater risk and governmental instability in Latin

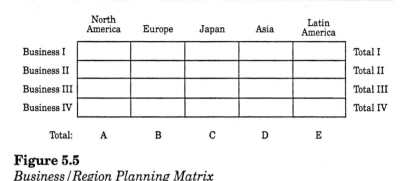

	North America	Europe	Japan	Asia	Latin America	
Business I						Total I
Business II						Total II
Business III						Total III
Business IV						Total IV
Total:	A	B	C	D	E	

Figure 5.5
Business / Region Planning Matrix

America despite the higher margins. These debates are inevitable and natural in international business. The task of management is to foster the problem-solving climate, mediate issues, and, as a last resort, break ties so that the plan can be implemented. It is optimal to force these debates to take place before the company commits to its plan for the period, in a data-based and mediated climate. This allows the managers to go on maneuvers before using live ammunition.

The result of successful completion of the planning process is that both regional and business managers have the same goals. The North American manager and the Business I manager share the goals for Business I in North America for the planning period. They can be jointly accountable for their accomplishment. The planning process is designed to achieve compatibility across the dimensions of the organization. When management has built an information system and can manage the planning process, it has created a multidimensional capability (Taylor, 1991). Percy Barnavick of ABB has created 1500 profit centers for businesses and countries. He claims to manage them through a matrix like the one shown in Fig. 5.6.

In summary, the planning process is a key to managing multidimensional strategies successfully. The process, when successfully conducted, resolves the inevitable conflicts and provides a forum for representatives of various dimensions to influence the company's direction. Independently of whatever dimension constitutes the organizational hierarchy, the company can respond to changes originating from multiple sources. Successful management of the planning process is based on extending the capabilities of the lateral organization into managing conflict at the top of the organization.

The Reward System

Once having developed an information system and a planning process, the next step in implementing the multidimensional plan is to use the planned outcomes as a basis for rewarding, or at least evaluating, performance. Historically, geographically organized companies have measured the North American manager only on profits in North America (Total A in Fig. 5.5), independently of the performance of any of the businesses. Companies organized by worldwide businesses measured the Business I manager only on profits for the business (Total I), independently of the performance in any country. This single, clear target was a motivating goal for the single-dimension hierarchical manager.

The reward system for multidimensional strategies is less clear and more multidimensional. It is not total profit in the region but meeting all planned targets that is the basis for evaluating the regional manager. The reward systems become more subjective. The negotiating process is continuous as targets change. The reward system lacks the clarity and focus of the single-dimensional reward and measurement system. But the single-dimension approach lacks the capability of cooperativeness and responsiveness needed for a multidimensional world. What was a strength in a simple unidimensional world is dysfunctional in a multidimensional world.

The reward system, planning process, and informational system form an integrated package. The reward system is based on the goals produced by the planning process; the planning process requires an information system to provide data upon which the plan is created. The combination creates a multidimensional capability for the organization and a vehicle through which integrators can exercise influence.

Responsibilities

Another method for creating a power base for the integrator role is to assign to it specific decision responsibilities and authority.

An indispensable tool for assigning responsibility and authority is the responsibility chart (Galbraith, 1973, Chapter 8). The negotiation process teaches people the situation and clarifies the roles and responsibilities of the integrators. The integrator role, if new, needs this kind of clarification and legitimizing. A major source of problems and conflicts in multidimensional organizations is a lack of clarity concerning responsiblity.

Budgets

Another method for enhancing an integrating role is to give it control over budgets. The designer can designate which budget categories and how much budget authority the integrator has. By having control of a budget and the ability to write checks on it, the integrator can exercise influence.

Product managers in consumer goods companies have budget control over advertising, promotions, and sales contests. The budget authority is limited, but it gives the product manager the ability to maneuver in the marketplace. Worldwide product managers typically control product development budgets in high R&D investing industries. Thus, the integrators can be given selective budget authority over issues that require interunit coordination.

Dual Authority

A final step in increasing the power base of an integrator is to grant the role the ability to evaluate people in the hierarchy who work on their product, business, or market. As shown in Fig. 5.6, a person is identified as representing the integrator in each organizational unit. This person, called the subproject manager in the figure, is jointly evaluated by the unit manager and the integrator. This step creates the formal two-boss system of the matrix organization.

The two-boss system creates an organization based on dual authority. Such an organization is based on two equally important strategic dimensions, such as projects and functions in aerospace. The usual method of representing the organization is with a dotted line to the integrator, as shown in Fig. 5.6.

The dotted line to the project manager (integrator) from the subproject manager indicates dual authority. When it is successful, dual authority usually means that the manager with two

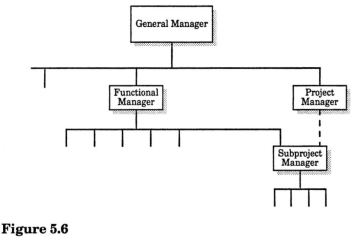

Figure 5.6
Matrix Structure with Dual Authority

bosses is jointly selected by them. The two managers also jointly set goals, and jointly evaluate the manager. All these supporting processes are necessary to employ dual authority successfully.

The two-boss structure remains controversial. Many managers believe that it cannot work and that it causes too much conflict. These observations are usually true in organizations that have not built a lateral capability but implement a matrix structure anyway. Managers in these organizations spend most of their time arguing over dotted and solid lines. Matrix success is not based on structure or dotted lines. It is based on the ability to manage conflict, set goals, and jointly evaluate people. These are skills that are built by developing the lateral organizational capability.

Another reason for difficulty with matrix organizations is that they may be unclear or overly complicated. The structure shown in Fig. 5.6 is ideal. There is only one level between the manager with two bosses and the general manager, or tie breaker. The general manager can call everyone who is "in the matrix" into a room and resolve a conflict. In contrast, the organizations that failed have had multinational matrix structures with four or five levels between the tie breaker and the two-boss manager. There are several hundred people who are located around the world in the matrix structure. There is no way to make this kind of structure function effectively.

The two-boss manager, called the subproject manager, is clearly identified in Fig. 5.6. That person and no one else in that function reports to the project manager. The other people in the function report to the subproject manager. The matrix is clear and well defined. When multiple people in a unit report to two people, the situation can become confusing and dysfunctional. Thus, the matrix should be simple and clear.

Much of the controversy also disappears when evaluation processes become a collective responsibility and peer evaluations are included. Evaluations are increasingly being performed by groups of managers (as in the example of the investment banks in Chapter 3). They are often based on subjective inputs given by managers, peers, subordinates, customers, and others. These evaluations provide a total assessment of overall performance and reduce the polarization of the two-boss, two-evaluation process.

The matrix organization remains a controversial management structure. However, when management has built a lateral capability, can manage conflict, and designs clear and simple structures, matrix organizations can provide significant flexibility to the company.

But I Thought Matrix Didn't Work

All of our discussion about integrators has sounded suspiciously like matrix organization. Many companies claim to have used matrix when using integrators. The author has always defined matrix as the two-boss version of the integrating role (Galbraith, 1973, 1977). The integrating role can also be used without a two-boss structure. But even some of the integrating roles have been problematic.

Over the past 20 years, the author has worked with many companies designing lateral organizations. As a result, I have arrived at a slightly different view of lateral, or matrix-type, organizations than is expressed in recent management books. In one sense, I have observed many failures. About seven in ten matrix organizations fail to achieve their goals, one in ten is marginal, and two in ten succeed. Based on these observations, my view is that it is wrong to say that matrix does not work. In many cases, it is successful in meeting its goals. I believe that most managements have failed at matrix. Most of the failures have occurred in companies that had poor voluntary organizations and poor relations between units. In spite of having no lateral capability, they installed a matrix anyway. They were soon overwhelmed by the conflict generated from trying to manage multiple dimensions simultaneously. The experience of these managers is that matrix does not work. They tried it and experienced great difficulty.

But two out of ten examples did succeed. Matrix succeeds where, over time, companies have built the capability described in these chapters. Other companies are building the capability today. These companies use terms like lateral organization, horizontal organization, and multidimensional strategies. But ten years ago, these concepts were called matrix.

In any case, the need for this multidimensional capability is greater today than it was ten years ago. The good news is that companies are building the capability within business units and in international areas. The capability still needs building at the corporate level. The building of these capabilities is a competitive necessity and, in some cases, it will give a company a significant competitive advantage.

Integrator Influence

All—or some combination of—the policies discussed in this chapter can give an integrating role a power base from which to influence lateral coordination. If they are implemented, the integrator role can be transformed from a weak staff role to a peer of the hierarchical roles. The strength of the integrating role will vary with the need for lateral coordination which, in turn, varies with the strategies shown in Table 2.2. Another way to represent the types and amounts of lateral organization is shown in Fig. 5.7. Represented along the vertical axis is the relative power distribution between the two strategic dimensions. The type of lateral organization is shown on the horizontal axis. The left half of the diagram represents a geographic organization structure across which business lateral organization forms are overlayed. The

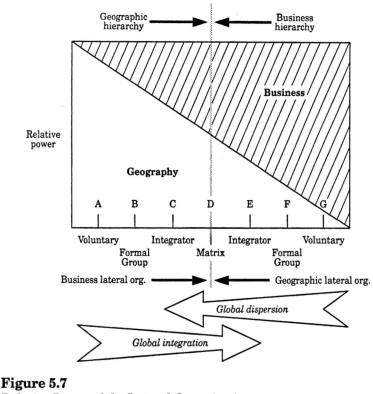

Figure 5.7
Relative Power of the Lateral Organization

right half represents a worldwide business organization structure across which geographic lateral forms are overlaid.

Different points along the horizontal axis represent different power distributions across the two-dimensional structure. Point A represents a geographic profit center organization structure with voluntary coordination of businesses across the countries and regions. Almost all power is exercised from the geographic standpoint. There is little global integration of businesses. Point B represents an increase in the power of the businesses by the formation of formal business groups. Still, the power structure is dominated by the geographies. Point C represents the creation of business integrators in the geographic structure. The Colgate-Palmolive structure shown in Fig. 5.3 is an example. Country and regional managers are still the profit centers, and the power distribution is tilted toward them. Then, through the use of the mechanisms described in this chapter, the power base of the business manager can be increased until point D is reached. At point D there is a power balance which represents the dual structures of a matrix organization as shown in Fig. 5.7. In essence, there are two line organizations in the matrix structure.

To the right of point D, the structure of the organization is built around business profit centers. All activities in countries and regions report to the business managers. The country and regional managers are integrators. Their strength can be varied by the same mechanisms described in this chapter. The area to the right of point E and continuing to point F represents the use of geographic formal groups overlaid on the business profit center structure. By now, almost all power in the organization is wielded by business managers. Finally, point G represents voluntary coordination within a country or region across the businesses that operate in the areas. Thus, there is continuum of power which can be distributed from 100 percent geographic through various distributions until it has shifted 100 percent to worldwide businesses. The organization designer can shift the power distribution by employing various types and amounts of lateral organization.

The power distribution shown in Fig. 5.7 will be shifted when strategic changes are required. As shown, the greater the need for global integration of a business, the farther to the right the designer would move the business. For example, as Colgate-Palmolive experienced increasing R&D intensity in its businesses, it moved from point A to point C to obtain greater integration of businesses across countries. The Japanese electronics companies operated at point G on the chart and exported around the world. By the end of the 1980s they had moved to point E. The change in the value of the yen, and threatened and real protectionism, caused them to disperse manufacturing activities around the world.

When companies feel strong pressure for both global dispersion and global integration, they operate somewhere between points C and E. This area represents the full multidimensional organization. The power will shift as the economic forces cause changes to the strategies of integration and dispersion. Shifts in strategic emphasis will result in shifts in the balance of power. An advantage will accrue to companies that can operate effectively as a multidimensional organization. Those companies will gain the strategic flexibility needed in many globally changing industries.

A similar argument could be made for distributions of power at the corporate or business-unit level. Figure 5.8 shows

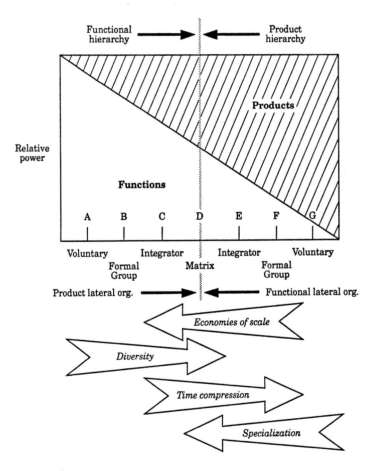

Figure 5.8
Business-Unit Power Distribution

the power distribution for a business unit consisting of functions and products (or projects or services). The strategy variables of product diversity and time compression will move the organization to the right and shift power to those who focus on products.

When employing resources with a high degree of specialization and economies of scale, there are pressures to manage these resources from a functional point of view. These forces move the organization toward more functional power (to the left on the diagram). Equal strategic imperatives force the business unit to operate between points C and E as a multidimensional business unit. Most aerospace companies operate in the area between points C and E.

Summary

Some strategies require that organizations employ full-time integrators to assist the general manager in coordinating across organizational units. This chapter described how to develop people who are effective in these kinds of roles. It also discussed ways to create a power base from which these people can work effectively. It concluded with a diagram to aid the organization designer in matching types and amounts of lateral organization with the coordination requirements of the strategy.

The integrating role is the most costly and complex form of lateral organization. It is most costly because it involves creating new, full-time management positions. It is also costly because these roles are employed in addition to formal groups and the voluntary organization. Integrating roles are complex because they generate conflict. People see the world differently when viewing it from different dimensions. Indeed, the purpose of the multidimensional organization is to see the world in its entirety, but from different perspectives. In order to manage the resulting conflict, the organization needs people who can manage the process, an information system to keep people knowledgeable, and a planning process for making the conflicts visible and manageable.

The chapter also continued the theme of building a lateral organizational capability. The building of the capability should now be seen as a cumulative process. By building a capability for the informal, voluntary organization, a company lays the groundwork for moving on to the more complicated formal groups. By building a capability for managing formal groups, a company lays the foundation for the use of integrators. When able to manage the multidimensional organization with integrating roles, the company will find that is has built a complete lateral capability. That capability gives the company the flexibility to respond to threats and opportunities from many sources. It is the most flexible form of organization.

In the next chapter, a popular variation on the integrating role is presented. This variation is the distributed organization. The case of SKF is used to illustrate the distributed organization for managing its European businesses.

6

The Distributed Organization

The last chapter discussed the multidimensional organization. This type of organization is created when integrating roles are added to coordinate activities across the hierarchical units; that is, the hierarchy is structured on one dimension, such as geography, and integrators who are focused on businesses coordinate activities across countries. There is a group of country managers and another group of business managers, each focused on their respective strategic dimensions. An alternative model, the two-hat model, was introduced for a pharmaceutical lab. This two-hat model is the distributed organization; that is, the alternative dimensions are not created as separate roles, but are distributed to the existing hierarchical managers, who then play two roles.

In this chapter, the distributed organization is discussed in more detail. Like other organizational forms, the distributed organization has both positive and negative features. The designers need to be aware of these features when making trade-off design decisions. Then, the international distributed organization is presented along with a case study of SKF, the Swedish bearing manufacturer. Finally, other examples of this pervasive form are described.

The Distributed Organization Model

An organization becomes distributed when headquarters' activities or missions are distributed from headquarters to be performed in operating units. The operating unit then has responsibility for the organization-wide mission, as well as its own operating responsibility. Thus the operating unit has a dual responsibility and its management wears two hats. The question is, "Why is the distributed organization increasingly the organization of choice among organizational designers?"

The headquarters model arose when the organization centralized activities that required scale and expertise. By placing an activity at headquarters, the activity is performed in one place for the entire organization. The central activity achieves scale and eliminates duplication. The reporting relationship to headquarters gives the unit a global perspective, a possible long-run perspective, and a neutral position to serve equally all units needing its service. Information systems, purchasing, R&D, and training are all examples of activities that may be centralized at headquarters to get neutral scale and expertise.

The negatives of the headquarters model are well known. Because it is centralized, the headquarters unit does not have the same sense of urgency to serve the local units. It provides a standard service to different local units. It often loses touch with the business and becomes skilled at abstract expertise instead. The local unit often acquires its own unit and performs the activity better. The debate between local units and headquarters is between centralization and decentralization. Decentralization results when the central unit is broken up and the fragmented units are placed in each local unit. Each local unit gains control of its own unit, but the company loses scale. The distributed organization results when the entire central unit is placed in one of the local units. The local unit serves its own needs and those of other local units. The distributed organization has aspects of both centralization and decentralization. But what is the advantage of the distributed organization?

The distributed organization arises when local expertise is superior to central expertise. For example, one of the business units of a corporation may buy large volumes of semiconductors and know the market well. Instead of centralizing buying for scale, why not let the business unit buy for the entire corporation? National accounts provides another example. Sales and service organizations are usually organized on a geographic basis. The result is that multiple sales offices will have General Motors or Procter & Gamble as a customer. For efficiency, these national accounts could be served out of a national accounts unit at headquarters. However, the Cincinnati sales office deals with

Procter & Gamble every day and knows them better than a central unit located elsewhere. Therefore, the national responsibility for Procter & Gamble is located in Cincinnati and the one for General Motors is in Detroit. These sales offices sell to all local customers and coordinate sales at all sales offices serving national accounts. In this way, the company retains the scale or single interface with a customer and gets local expertise and responsiveness.

Another factor resulting in the distributed organization is the trend toward reducing the size of corporate staffs. It is politically appealing to move an activity to a local operating unit and claim to have reduced staff for the benefit of constituencies who favor small, lean staffs. There is also an interest in improving service. Central staffs can become disinterested in local service and may lack a sense of urgency. If an operation moves to a local unit, under an operating manager, the unit will be more responsive and more service minded.

The distributed organization is also more politically attractive when changing from single- to multidimensional organization. In the last chapter, the example of Colgate-Palmolive was described. Colgate introduced integrators who managed worldwide categories across countries. Initially, the strong country managers were not enthusiastic about sharing responsibilities with the new managers. Another option would have been for the country with the most effective oral care products to assume worldwide responsibility. Another strong country with a good toiletries business could assume worldwide responsibility for the toiletries category. In this way, with many country managers sharing facets of worldwide responsibility, there would be less resistance. There will also be less resistance when increasing or decreasing the power base of a dimension if it is shared with other dimensions in hierarchical roles. If decisions about R&D are taken from country managers and given to business managers, there will be less resistance if a business and country responsibility are lodged in the same role. The change amounts to a reshuffling of responsibilities among members of a constituency, not the removal of responsibility to a new constituency. So a distributed model can be a more flexible model when shifting priorities from one dimension to another. There are no losers in the power shift.

The distributed model can also increase the motivation of a local unit. It is a compliment to be selected for an organization-wide role. It is motivating to receive an enhanced role and more responsibility. The distributed organization gives local units a stake in the company's performance.

There are some negatives in the distributed model. The main issue is the loss of neutrality of an organization-wide service. A central unit at headquarters took a company-wide view and served all units equally. Now, one of the local units provides the service for everyone. What is to keep the local unit from serving its needs first and best? The other units may get second class service. Before, the local unit was dependent on headquarters. Now, it is dependent on a fellow local unit. In both cases, the local unit has no control over the service it receives—but at least headquarters was unbiased.

A central unit at headquarters often takes a longer perspective. Long-term commitments (to R&D funding, for example) are needed to build technical capability. Similar investments may be needed in training or information technology. If the activity is placed in an operating unit, the long-term perspective may be lost. If the operating unit experiences budget problems, it may cut back on the company-wide service in order to meet its short-run goals. The long-run focus and the objective focus were the benefits of a headquarters-reporting relationship.

The usual method of eliminating the negatives of the distributed organization is to choose policies for the other organizational dimensions that are represented in the Star Model shown in Chapter 1. They can be chosen so as to counteract the problems listed here. In other words, budgeting can still be centralized and not subject to short-run cuts, even if the activity is executed in an operating unit. The operating unit may be required to have a separate plan for the shared activity. The performance goals in the plan will become performance measures for the operating unit. The satisfaction of other units with the service may be surveyed and weighed in making performance evaluations of the operating unit. The activity may be staffed with people from all operating units on rotating assignments. These and other types of policies can allow the organization to capture the positives of the distributed organization while minimizing the negatives. These policies will be discussed in the next section, using the SKF case with specific reference to the international area.

The International Distributed Organization

The distributed organization is being implemented throughout the corporation. But it is in the area of international business that it is being applied extensively (Bartlett and Goshal, 1989). The distributed organization in the international context is referred to as the trans-national organization. There are a number of factors that are causing companies to choose to implement it.

In the international arena, the distributed organization is seen as a solution to the dual demands of global integration and global dispersion. Pressures for global integration are believed to be continuing due to increased investments in R&D and intangible assets. In addition, several factors are driving more global dispersion. More and more companies are moving value-adding activities out of the country of ownership and locating them in the "best" country for their execution.

The first factor driving dispersion is the oldest factor. Many countries are using access to their market as a lever to force companies to locate manufacturing and product development activities in their country and, if possible, to export to other countries. If a company wants to sell its products in France, it will probably have to make and design some of them in France. Indonesia, India, and China all are aware that the size of their populations make them attractive, high-volume markets. As a result, their governments all require local manufacturing and technology transfer in order to have access to their markets. Thus, as market access becomes the scarce commodity, more governments will negotiate with companies to add value in their country in order to have access to their market.

Even if countries were not forcing companies to disperse their activities, the companies would likely move them out of countries of ownership. The days when the United States had the most advanced markets and technologies are over. As a result, companies are moving their business headquarters to the country where the most advanced markets and technologies are located. If U.S. companies are not waging strategic battles in leading-edge markets today, they will not be prepared when the heavy hitters come to compete on our home turf tomorrow. Procter & Gamble finds that the most advanced market for detergents is Germany. Germany has the most advanced Green movement and the toughest competitors in Henkel and Deutsche Unilever. The most advanced market for paper products is Japan. Kao is leading the way with new products. The products introduced in Tokyo today will be introduced in San Francisco tomorrow. Oral care is most advanced in the United States. Procter & Gamble therefore concludes that it must locate strategy and product-design responsibility for those businesses in the most advanced markets. It is necessary to have the business leadership located in—and competing in—the leading markets. Thus, many companies are locating their business headquarters in countries where the business is facing its most demanding customers and toughest competitors. Even without protectionist threats, value-adding activities are being dispersed around the world.

Finally, activities are being located where the skills are located. Some societies are outstanding at performing certain work. Italians and Scandinavians have superior design talents. Indians and Chinese are superior at certain kinds of mathematics and, therefore, software development. Russian scientists are now doing R&D for Sun Micro Systems. Digital Equipment Corporation located an R&D facility in Israel. Miniaturization is a scarce and desired skill. The Japanese excel at it, but so do the Swiss. Disc-drive manufacturers are locating facilities in Neuchatel, Switzerland, and hiring technicians who are leaving the mechanical watch industry. Companies are searching for skills everywhere and trying to secure a competitive advantage any way they can.

Thus, companies are moving value-adding activities and responsibilities to different parts of the world in order to acquire access to markets, compete in the most advanced markets, and utilize the best talents. As a result, companies are experiencing a dispersion of the activities at the same time that they are experiencing a need to integrate them. The distributed organization is a way to organize and achieve both integration and dispersion. The next section describes how SKF created and manages its European distributed organization.

SKF: A Case Study

SKF, the Swedish bearing manufacturer, was like many of its European counterparts. Motivated primarily by a small domestic market, they expanded internationally in the early 1900s. However, the first half of the century was dominated by two world wars and very high tariff barriers. As a result, each country's subsidiary had to be entirely self-sufficient; that is, it had to produce all products for its country market. There were no cross-border shipments of products within Europe. The Swedish subsidiary developed new product technology, and transferred that know-how to its subsidiaries in Europe. The subsidiaries nevertheless remained self-contained; only the Swedish company could export to interested countries ouside of Europe. The organization structure was based on country profit centers and is shown in Fig. 6.1. This system worked well and was used by most European companies.

Things began to change in the 1970s. The Japanese entered the market and began to capture market share. The Japanese used focused factories and entered the low end of the market with very much cheaper products. The bearing business is very capital- and R&D-intensive. About 10 percent of the products are new each year. Because bearing companies sell to the global automobile and machine-tool manufacturers, the business would have been a globally integrated one, even if it had been created in a business environment with no tariff barriers. The duplicate and low-scale facilities in each country in the era of GATT and free trade put SKF at a disadvantage against the

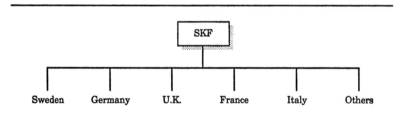

Figure 6.1
Typical European Country Structure

Japanese. They then began a strategic change, integrating the business throughout Europe and dispersing pan-European missions to each country subsidiary. SKF used the new product development process to evolve to the integrated business strategy and organization. They assigned each new product to be developed and manufactured in only one country. This country would supply all of the other country markets with that product. The subsidiary would also have the responsibility to export to other countries around the world. If the first new product went to Germany, the second one went to France. The third product went to the U.K. and the fourth to Italy. In this manner, each country acquired a product responsibility to develop, manufacture, and export to the other countries.

The distribution of pan-European product responsibilities greatly lowered costs by eliminating duplication in each country and achieving scale by manufacturing in only one country. This focusing of factories stopped the erosion of market share. Also, each country became an equal partner in the business. The creation of the distributed organization shifted the structure from that of a parent-child model to one of peers, as shown in Figs. 6.2 and 6.3.

The parent-child model concentrates all strategy and product development in the country of ownership. Once developed, the products are transferred to the subsidiaries for execution. Thus all the important decisions are made at headquarters. The subsidiaries feel like just that—subsidiary, or second class. The peer model arises as pieces of headquarters' responsibility are moved to the other countries. Each country has a portion of the company headquarters. Each country becomes an equal player. Each makes strategy and develops products that the other countries implement. The movement to multiple headquarters motivates the subsidiaries, provides attractive work, and enables them to attract talent.

The countries like the distributed organization. It locates valuable work and jobs in their country. It provides them with exports. It also requires them to import product from the other countries. But the value-added work is used as the quid pro quo.

There are also some negatives associated with the new organization. There is usually some resistance at headquarters. Many of the interesting responsibilities that are moving to the

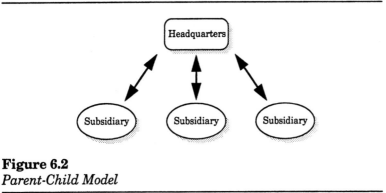

Figure 6.2
Parent-Child Model

countries are being taken from the headquarters. Some of the people will move with the responsibility. The old structure consisted of autonomous, self-sufficient subsidiaries. Each subsidiary controlled the supply of product to its customers. Now the French subsidiary is dependent on the German and British subsidiaries to supply some products to French customers. There is the question of whether the German subsidiary will give first priority to its German customers. What happens when supply is short or problems with quality occur? SKF has worked out several approaches to the dependence issue.

The distributed organization works best when dependence is *balanced* and *reciprocal*. At SKF, each subsidiary was roughly the same in size and effectiveness; no one unit was dominant. They were equally balanced, so a peer-to-peer relationship could be used. When one of the units is very large or one is very weak, cooperation is likely to break down. Cooperation is based on reciprocity; there is mutual dependence. The German subsidiary is as dependent on the French as the French subsidiary is on the Germans. SKF has fostered a norm of reciprocity. "I'll take care of your customers and you take care of mine." So it is balance, symmetry, and reciprocity that holds the peer countries together.

SKF has taken lateral coordination a few steps further. One of the features of the distributed organization is that it creates communication complexity. In the parent-child model, the communication pattern is between a subsidiary and headquar-

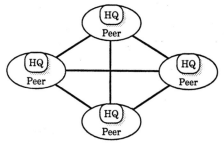

Figure 6.3
Peer-to-Peer Model

ters. The pattern is simple and one-to-one. The pattern in the peer model is that every subsidiary communicates with every other subsidiary. With multiple headquarters, each subsidiary must communicate with all of them. The distributed organization is a communication-intensive model.

The communication needs have been met at SKF by creating a communication network for its two main business processes. The core processes are the product supply and the new product development processes. They have created both a formal information technology network and an interpersonal network to match the communication needs.

The supply function has been facilitated by a worldwide information system that tracks all products in all countries. SKF standardized all subsidiaries on IBM equipment and built the integrated logistics system with satellites and common equipment. Thus information technology plays a big role in establishing the distributed organization.

The supply function also is carried out by an integrating department which performs the forecasting, scheduling, factory loading, and inventory control. This unit schedules all the factories in the subsidiaries. The scheduling unit is located in Belgium. There are no factories in Belgium, so the unit is likely to be objective and unbiased in its decisions. The Swedes understand the power of neutrality. The unit is run by a Swede with long experience in scheduling. Half of the unit is staffed with

Belgians who are permanent, long-term employees. They provide experience and a memory for the function. The other half of the unit is staffed with high-potential employees from the subsidiaries on two-year rotating assignments. They bring knowledge and personal contacts from the situation from which they came. They will know, for example, to plan a lighter schedule in Germany on Monday because it is the first day of the hunting season and absenteeism will be high. Thus the unit produces scheduling decisions based on complete and neutral knowledge.

The scheduling unit recreates the European business in microcosm. The total situation can be represented among a small group of people who can reach optimum decisions. They can draw on the formal, detailed quantitative data from the telecom system. They can draw on the qualitative judgments and local experience of the participants. The experience provides good training for the high-potential subsidiary managers. It gives SKF an opportunity to see them in a pan-European setting. They can observe who can best think on a pan-European basis. The participants develop relationships that they can use on a voluntary basis for cross-subsidiary communications. Thus the neutral supply function is a clever integrating device that both builds the lateral organizational capability and schedules the distributed factories.

The second communication network is built around the R&D function. The R&D laboratory is located in Holland near the University of Utrecht. Again, Holland is a country that does not have a factory and is therefore neutral in allocating product responsibilities to countries that do have factories. The laboratory is staffed on the same basis as the supply function. Roughly half the personnel are permanent, long-term residents of Holland. The remainder are engineers from the factory that was chosen to develop and manufacture the products. These engineers came to develop new products at the laboratory and take the product back to the factory. The products are developed using pan-European teams, with marketing representatives from many countries. While at the laboratory, they learn the pan-European market requirements while developing the product. They meet and establish relationships with the laboratory personnel, and they establish relationships with other engineers from other factories. Thus the laboratory creates new technologies, develops new products, and also builds the lateral organization.

The key features of the SKF distributed organization are the balance and reciprocity among the subsidiaries and the neutral integrating units for the core processes. Several other major changes were also implemented to complete the new organization. The criteria for selecting country managers and their measurement and evaluation had to be completely changed. Also the entire management style for the company had to be altered.

Under the parent-child model, the country managers needed to be knowledgeable only about their own country. An Englishman ran the U.K. subsidiary and a Frenchman ran the French subsidiary. They had very little contact with other country managers. They were independent and concerned only with their own profitability. They controlled all the resources to meet that bottom line and wanted no interference from headquarters. Under the distributed model, the country managers still had profit responsibility for the country, but had supply and product development responsibility for all of Europe. Local, provincial country managers would be replaced by manager's capable of thinking and acting on a pan-European basis. They needed to understand the Italian and German customer as well as their own. They needed to be team players, to influence without authority, and to communicate with other managers in other countries. Communication and language skills are needed, even though SKF adopted English as the company language. Thus, the distributed organization requires a very different kind of manager.

In the short term, several country managers had to be replaced by Swedes. Over time, the lateral organization creates the managers to run countries. Those managers who rotate through the supply function and R&D, who work on product teams, and who communicate across countries will rise to country manager roles.

The measurement and evaluation system had to be changed to reflect the pan-European responsibilities. The former country manager was measured solely on his country's profitability. The new country manager is measured on country profitability, pan-European product profitability, and teamwork within Europe. A matrix like the one shown in Fig. 5.5 was created to plan and measure profits. The evaluation was then subjective, because managers did not control all of the factors contributing to their profit measures. The evaluation changed from a clear, measurable, and controllable country profit goal to several less-controllable goals. Plus, the managers were assessed on their teamwork and communication skills. The rewards and measurements are more numerous and more ambiguous in the distributed organization. The managers need to be comfortable with this situation.

The distributed organization also creates challenges for the manager who is to lead it. Under the parent-child model, the leader deals with country managers one-on-one. He or she can make a series of separate deals with them. Others may not even know or care what agreements were reached with other country managers. Under the distributed organization, the leader must manage a team. The countries are all interdependent. Decisions need to be jointly taken. There is much more communication. There is much more debate and conflict to be managed. The old one-on-one style will undermine teamwork. The distributed organization is more collegial and requires group goals, rewards, and bonuses. Bonuses are granted on Europe-wide performance.

In summary, the design of the distributed organization involves much more than merely moving a headquarters responsibility to a local unit. The distribution of responsibilities escalates the level of interdependence between local units. It requires much greater levels of communication, coordination, and teamwork. It is greatly enhanced by modern information technology, as it also requires interpersonal networks. The planning and measurement systems all need to reflect the multidimensional nature of the team responsibility. The people all need to be selected and developed on teamwork and communication skills. Teamwork also needs to start at the top. The leader needs to manage a team and show the way for the rest of the organization. SKF has successfully implemented the distributed organization. They have aligned all of the organizational dimensions in the Star Model among themselves and with the pan-European strategy.

Other Distributed Organizations

The distributed organization is being adopted in other parts of the company, as well as in international areas. All of these applications require the same design thoroughness as SKF applied to its European operations.

The Corporation

The corporation is distributing corporate-wide responsibilities to business units. The two most prominent examples are distributed staffs and Centers of Competency. Earlier, it was mentioned that companies are reducing the size of the corporate staff. Some activities are eliminated and others are contracted out. Still others are distributed to the business units. The business unit then uses the corporate staff activity to serve its needs and those of the corporation as a whole. For example, Hughes Aircraft is eliminating the corporate training staff. Most of them are moving to the Group level where they will join the Group staff, which has the best training unit. Recruiting is moving to the business unit that already hires the most engineers. Mars, Inc., and Emerson Electric have operated with distributed staffs for years.

Other corporate activities are being moved to business units, or a business unit's capability is being expanded to a corporate capability. The focus and emphasis on core competency and capabilities are leading corporations to take inventory of their skill areas. They are benchmarking them against those of other companies. The capabilities that are unique and/or superior are being designated as corporate core capabilities. The business unit with the largest or most advanced unit executing the capability is designated as the Center of Competency (or Center of Excellence or Center of Responsibility). The business unit is responsible for the corporate-wide development, deployment, and execution of the capability.

The same principles of effectiveness apply to the corporation. The activities will be shared effectively when businesses are *balanced* and dependence is *mutual*. Reciprocity holds the system together. Coordinating units, even when located in a business unit, receive corporate funding, corporate-wide staffing, and corporate measures of performance. For these reasons, the distributed organization violates business-unit autonomy. And it should. The resources are corporate resources, not business-unit resources. People with electronic imaging skills at Kodak are free to move across businesses. The manager responsible for the capability and counterparts in other business units are to allocate people across the corporation.

The distributed staff and Centers of Competency require a corporate lateral organization capability. The manager responsible for the center is the integrator across the corporation. That manager and counterparts in other units form a Competency Council. Experts in the competency are to form their own interpersonal networks throughout the corporation. As they move to various assignments, they rotate across all business units. The Competency Council invests in a competency data base to be shared across business units. Corporate management receives the council's plans and goals. The council receives corporate funding. The council evaluates all personnel in the competency. Each of these features needs to be developed for each competence. Collectively, they form the lateral organizational capability of the corporate level.

Business Units

At various places within business units, the distributed organization is being implemented. National or global accounts were described earlier. The same structures are used in service organizations that are geographically organized and serve clients in multiple locations. Banks, consultants, accounting firms, and investment banks all use distributed responsibility for large, multilocation clients.

The distributed organization is being extended to factories. The flexible factory allows the business to locate factories closer to the customer and to serve all their needs. However, a business does not want to duplicate overhead at every plant. Instead, each plant gets a responsibility for a particular function, such as computer-aided manufacturing, software development and maintenance, electronic maintenance, or training. All the plants are linked with E-mail and video conferencing. Personnel will arrive within 24 hours at a plant requesting service.

Each of these examples also requires a complete organization design. Again, the design must incorporate balance, mutuality, reciprocity, intense lateral communication, employee rotation, management overview and review, and integrated shared data bases. When all of these factors are present and aligned, the company gets the majority of the benefits of the distributed organization and few of the negatives.

Summary

Many companies are choosing to implement the distributed organization, which is a type of lateral organization. This chapter described the forces that are causing companies to implement the international version. The SKF example described all the supporting changes that need to accompany the distribution of an activity in order to make the organization design complete. These changes led to the use of balance and reciprocity as key features of the distributed model. Finally, some other examples were given where the distributed organization is becoming popular. In all of these areas, the same complete design is required. Also needed is the information technology to facilitate the intense communication that is required to make distributed organizations function effectively.

7

Lateral Coordination Cases

In this chapter, a couple of case examples are analyzed to illustrate and reinforce the ideas presented in the earlier chapters. The first example is Dow-Corning, which has been using a multidimensional organization for over 25 years and has built a lateral organizational capability over that time period. The second example is a young Hewlett-Packard division that rapidly built the same lateral organizational capability. In today's environment, companies do not have decades to acquire capabilities. The two cases will provide some contrasts and some similarities, which will recap the content of the book.

A Multidimensional Organization— Dow-Corning

Dow-Corning is well known for its successful execution of the multidimensional, or matrix, organization. Its story has been presented in several publications (Goggins, 1974; Galbraith and Kazanjian, 1986). In this section, the focus is on the design of the business boards as the key lateral organization, and on capability-building to sustain the boards.

Dow-Corning is organized on the concept of a "three-legged stool." The three legs are functions, businesses, and geographies. The structure is shown in Fig. 7.1. All of the people are assigned to the "functions" leg. As the company grows to over $1 billion in sales, the regions are becoming larger and more independent in their day-to-day operations. The structure could be redrawn with the regions as the basic profit center, con-

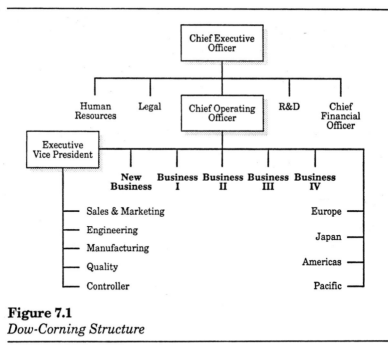

Figure 7.1
Dow-Corning Structure

sisting of functional departments. The structures for the United States and Europe (the largest portions of the business) are shown in Fig. 7.2.

The integration across functions within a region, and internationally across regions, takes place within the lateral business organization called the business board. There is a great deal of integrating to do: The company invests 8 percent of sales in R&D. Chemical processing is a capital-intensive business that produces universal products with some tailoring for local requirements. As approximately 35 percent of sales comes from new products introduced in the last five years, so there is a lot of new product development activity that needs to be coordinated across functions and across regions. The business strategy is high on product and market diversity, change, and time compression. The international strategy is high on both global dispersion and global integration. The lateral coordination is accomplished through extensive informal networks, formal groups (the busi-

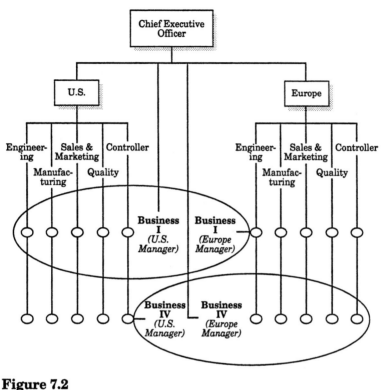

Figure 7.2
U.S. and European Structure

ness boards), and integrators called business managers. The next sections focus on the business boards, business managers, and human resources practices that build the lateral capability.

Business Board Structure

There are five business boards, with one devoted to new businesses. The business boards are both multidimensional and hierarchical in their structure. There are five boards in Europe, and the same five in the United States. These boards coordinate across functions within their region. They manage the day-today coordination across functions and the new product development activities that are assigned to them.

Each board consists of one, or sometimes two, managers from each function. A board usually includes five to six people and a business manager. The board members are all dedicated to the business full-time, and are physically located together. The engineering, marketing, controller, and quality managers all manage the business within their function; they are line managers from the function. The manufacturing managers, on the other hand, are all integrators within their function, but are dedicated to the business.

Each board member from a function also monitors five to six product lines within the business. In some cases, they will convene and chair a cross-functional product board. In addition, new product projects also report to the board members. There may be four or five projects at any one time. Each project is managed by a cross-functional team and a project leader. The project leader usually comes from engineering, but some come from marketing. Thus, there is a hierarchy of formal groups. There are 5 cross-functional business boards, there can be 5 or 6 product boards, and 20 to 25 cross-functional new product projects within a business. The projects are linked to the boards by having four to five projects and project leaders assigned to functional members of the business boards. The functional board member is, therefore, the key linking role in the hierarchical array of cross-functional groups.

The global integration is coordinated across regions by expanding the business board for a region into a global business board. If the United States is the largest and most advanced market for Business I, then the U.S. business manager would become the global business manager for Business I. The global business board could consist of the five or six functional members, plus the business managers from Europe and from any other region where Dow-Corning is involved in that business. In this way, the business managers are the links across regions for the global business boards.

If Europe is the largest and most advanced market for Business IV, the business manager and board from Europe become the global business board. The U.S. business manager becomes a member of the global board, as will other business managers from other regions. The U.S. business manager for Business I and the European business manager for Business IV report to the chief executive, rather than to their regional vice presidents. The regional business boards coordinate day-to-day activities. The global business boards focus on investments in plant and equipment and R&D, product development, and sourcing of products to markets. All of these decisions are reviewed by the management committee, consisting of all functional business and regional managers.

Thus, Dow-Corning coordinates its regional, functional structure with business boards. These boards are both multidimensional and hierarchical. There are both regional and global business boards that are linked by the business managers. Regional boards are subdivided into product boards and new product project teams. Each member of the business board is responsible for several project teams and team leaders. In this way, Dow-Corning links the many formal groups into a globally integrated business.

Business Managers

The business managers are integrators. All the company's employees are assigned to functions in the regions. Originally, no one reported to the business managers. But as the size of the divisions has increased, a few of the board members have come to manage activities that are totally dedicated to one business, and report to the business manager. The majority of board members, however, belong to a function. Thus the business managers have very little authority.

The business managers exercise influence primarily through the planning process. Dow-Corning has invested a great deal of time in creating an accounting system that supports all three legs of the stool. Costs can be assigned to businesses, products, functions, and regions. Fully 80 percent of the costs can be directly assigned to a business. There, those costs are controllable by the business boards. It is acknowledged that the business is the basic profit and loss center in a region. It is the business board that plans investments in capital and R&D. These plans set goals and targets, which become the basis for activity in the functions that execute the plans. Thus, there is a lateral organization for planning, and a line organization for doing.

The business manager is the leader of the business board. All board members are jointly evaluated by functional managers and business managers. A norm was established early on that gave the business manager 50 percent of the vote. Although boards do not vote, the norm means that the manager makes the decision when the board is deadlocked or cannot reach consensus. Thus, the business manager is influential in building the plan, which is executed by the functional organization. The influence is not unilateral. The board's plans are reviewed and discussed with functional and regional managers prior to becoming a fiscal commitment.

Thus, the business managers operate from a power base that is supported by several factors. The roles are high-status roles to which most managers aspire. The global business managers report to the chief executive. They participate in joint performance evaluations for their board members, who physically reside with them. But two additional features give them their substantial power. The first is the lead role in the planning process. This process integrates the three legs of the stool, and is based on a sophisticated multidimensional information system. The second feature is the development process used to create the business managers and the other top managers at Dow-Corning. They grow their own and, in the process, create a lateral organizational capability.

Human Resource Practices

The management at Dow-Corning is continuously developed from selection to assignment by the executive committee. The executive committee itself invests a lot of time and energy in managing the process. Ultimately, the process develops a manager who has broad general skills, is secure enough to manage conflict, can handle the ambiguity of a multidimensional organization, and is a team player. As these people are developed, the lateral organization is simultaneously developed.

The process begins with selection and self-selection. All of the managers are chemical engineers who have the potential to become the ideal manager and are willing to spend most of the rest of their lives in a small company town in northern Michigan. Most of the managers come from process engineering, and, specifically, from the scale-up function. It is no accident that scale-up is a source of generalists. Scale-up is an activity that takes new products and processes and refines them so that they can be transferred to the factory. It is an integrating activity that exists at the intersection of R&D and manufacturing. People who are successful at scale-up have the potential to become successful integrators. These engineers are then rotated and trained to play various roles in the lateral organization.

The rotation process was introduced in Chapter 3. It has the feature of providing variety and continuity. The new role provides new challenges for learning and at the same time retains enough continuity so that the engineer can contribute. The process strikes a balance between learning and contributing.

The process proceeds by having an engineer follow the product from scale-up into manufacturing. The product provides the continuity; the new manufacturing role provides the variety. From the factory in the United States, the engineer may transfer the product to a factory in Europe. Once the factory is established in Europe, the future manager may rotate to the controller role in that factory in Europe. And so it would continue, something old and something new in each role, as the manager rotates across functions and regions.

Experience is also provided on the third leg of the stool in the board activities. The manager first participates as a member of a new product project. Successful contributors become project leaders of the next new product project. Next they lead global product projects. Business board membership is the next rung on the lateral organizational ladder. A board member is simultaneously a member of a team (business board), leader of a team (product board), and developer of future integrators (product project leaders). The ladder is completed by moves to regional business manager and global business manager. Through these moves, from scale-up engineer, the business manager learns cross-functional teamwork, conflict management in other cultures, how to influence without authority, and general management skills.

Dow-Corning has made extensive use over the years of a consulting firm with skills in human resource practices. This firm has developed training programs in group problem solving, interpersonal-skill development, and conflict management. Managers take these courses prior to participating in project teams or boards. The firm also is continuously sensing, surveying, and counseling on issues that inevitably arise in a multidimensional organization. And, finally, the firm has worked with the company in developing, assessing, and selecting the kinds of people who will thrive in a global business integrated by business boards.

The managers who thrive are those who develop four characteristics. First, they must be team players. One manager said, "There are no stars here. Our culture is built around cross-functional teams. You get your worth by being part of something." Second, they must be able to deal with ambiguity. In a multidimensional organization, you may have two bosses and be working for a third on an assignment. The higher you go in the organization, the more ambiguous—but more flexible—are the roles. Third, they must be secure people. There is continual conflict when situations must be viewed from at least three perspectives. This conflict is a normal, natural part of the job. Insecure people escalate rather than resolve conflicts. They tie up too much time—their own and others—on simple decisions. And, finally, managers need broad general skills. At an executive committee meeting, the agenda could consist of a marketing opportunity in Europe, a manufacturing issue in Japan, an R&D discovery in the United States, and an investment in a plant serving four businesses. The development challenge is to select and develop these characteristics in the management corps.

The top management of the company manages the development process. In addition to working with the consulting firm and investing resources in rotation and training activities, management invests its own time in evaluating all people who are judged to be officer material. For one and a half weeks a year, the functional and regional managers review their organization and management talent with the executive committee. They discuss the next two levels of their organization. The purpose is to get collective input in the assessment of people who happen to be currently working for a particular manager.

The entire process is a personal network-building process. Rotation builds a manager's network. The successful managers are those who learn to use the network to get results. People are assessed and discussed who are successful, which further widens their possible contacts. As people develop, their personal networks develop. As the personal networks develop, the lateral organization develops.

Flexible and Multidimensional

Dow-Corning regards its multidimensionality as a real asset. The multiple dimensions guarantee that policy issues and conflicts get surfaced. In this way, more heads get focused on complex issues and collective input is provided.

The flexibility of the organization is another advantage. One manager said, "Being multidimensional allows you to do anything or organize around any issue. If you are divisionalized, you are limited." Dow-Corning continuously collects information about—and acts upon—issues concerning products, functions, businesses, and geographies. Their skill at lateral organization would permit them to coordinate across units on other issues as well. This flexible organization rests on the skills of general, flexible managers.

Summary

Dow-Corning has created a lateral organization consisting primarily of business boards and business managers. These business-focused groups coordinate across functions and geography. The lateral capability has been built and sustained over 25 years. The key features of the capability are the multidimensional information and planning system and the sophisticated rotation and management-development process. Neither of these features can be easily or quickly duplicated.

A New Hewlett-Packard Division*

In 1985, the Terminals Division at Hewlett-Packard found itself facing a substantially increased need for lateral coordination. Being two years old, it did not have 25 years of capability building to support the lateral organization. In the fast-moving electronics business, the division had to build the capability and use it simultaneously. The remainder of the chapter tells the story of how the division successfully and rapidly built its lateral organizational capability. The situation facing the division is described first. Then the substantial up-front planning and organizational development are described. The multidimensional and hierarchical structure of the teams is described next, followed by a discus-

---

*This is a disguised but true case.

sion of a number of techniques that supported the lateral organization.

The Situation in 1985

The Terminals Division was created in 1983 to design and produce terminals for Hewlett-Packard systems, low-end personal computers, and video display subsystems. It located away from Silicon Valley in order to reduce operating costs. Nevertheless, by 1985, the division was not competitive. It was losing market share. Its terminals were ranked high in quality, but were too expensive.

A new management team was appointed and was in place by 1985. They faced a choice of either sourcing terminals from the Far East, or radically changing their ways of doing business and manufacture at low cost in the United States. They chose the latter course, and launched a program to transform the division into a world-class, low-cost manufacturer.

Planning and Organization Development

A key feature of the process was the amount of front-end work devoted to developing skills and teams, and then the immediate use of those skills to plan the program. A second feature was the extensive communication to—and involvement of—all 1800 employees in creating the mission, plans, and objectives of the program.

Mission. The process began by simultaneously working on the mission for the division and developing trust and teamwork among the new management group. The division manager and his team worked with an outside consultant on a training program of team-building, consensus decision-making, and leadership for the new environment. The management team went through the program and also participated in H-P's in-house program, called Process of Management (POM). These education programs gave everyone a common set of tools and a common language.

The team then tackled the mission for the division. The mission emerged after several very intense sessions. The mission was:

> To *grow* the terminal business by becoming a *world*-class supplier, *lowest*-cost producer, and *highest*-quality provider.

Although the statement appeared to be a generic mission statement, there were some very substantial changes that were hotly debated. Recall that the business was losing market share. Now, according to the mission, the business was expected to remain the highest-quality provider, while becoming the lowest-cost producer. By virtue of this, it was also expected to grow and achieve global volume. Of these requirements, it is the "lowest-cost statement" that signified a major change. In 1985, Hewlett-Packard was good at doing many things. But being a market-driven, lowest-cost producer of commodity products was not one of them. H-P was good at designing and producing technology-driven, high-performance products at high margins, for sophisticated customers. The management team would have the dual task of changing the division and selling the mission to H-P management.

The management team felt that the experience and the training was very valuable. The process gave them a common language and some shared values, and it removed a number of barriers to communication in the new group. They got to know each other when arguing over the words in the mission statement. They began to understand their colleagues' ways of thinking, their values, and their emotions. But it also led to a common, shared purpose.

The process was then cascaded down the organization. All managers in the division went through the team-building and consensus decision-making program. All managers went through H-P's Process of Management Program. All managers participated in group sessions to understand and debate the mission statement. These sessions were led by members of the management team. The process extended the shared language and tools throughout the division. The management team then convened and issued the final mission statement. The effort sparked a sense of urgency throughout the division and achieved a shared, common purpose. H-P absolutely had to cut costs wherever possible while maintaining quality.

Planning. The next steps were to create a team for implementing the new, low-cost products and to plan the business and the new terminal products. A new program manager was appointed, who reported to both the R&D manager and the division manager. The new program manager then worked closely with the management team in staffing the new program team with 17 people.

The new program team was carefully selected. The people already employed at H-P were not necessarily those that were needed for a tightly built team effort. H-P had often recruited engineers with strong-willed, independent personalities. Heroes at H-P were often those who disobeyed management directives and then proved management to be wrong. These types were avoided, and the management team selected and attracted team players.

Special attention was devoted to selecting the program manager. He was a proven project leader on new products and had credibility with the design engineers. Additionally, he had a very low-key style and had good relationships with the other functions. He was also ready for a promotion.

The program team then began their own specific team-building efforts, simultaneously producing a program plan. The rest of the division management completed plans for the other product lines. Both groups followed the H-P planning process, which was taught in the POM Program. The planning process is a very disciplined process for creating a hierarchy of goals, beginning with the division general manager.

The division manager's goals are inferred from the strategy. Then, for each division manager goal there is a functional subgoal for each functional manager. For each subgoal that a functional manager has, a second level of subgoals is created for the direct reports of the functional manager. In this manner, a hierarchy of goals is cascaded down from each of the division manager's goals. The goals must be aligned across functions and levels of the structure. Much discussion and debate takes place around the goals. They must be aligned and measurable.

The planning effort produces considerable up-front discussion about what is to be done and who is to do it. These discussions also build on the consensus decision-making program. The result of the effort is a hierarchy of goals that produces alignment among functions. The process generates a set of functional goals and priorities that are consistent among themselves and with the mission.

These plans and goals for each function are placed on a single sheet of paper. It starts with the mission and the division objective, and develops the logic and reasons behind the functional objective. It places each piece of the business in the context of the overall strategy. These papers are posted throughout the area for each function. They are presented and discussed with all employees. The process represents an attempt to see that all employees know and understand their unit's goals and how they relate to the division's mission.

These goals also provide criteria for making trade-offs and resolving conflicts. Participants in teams will have been part of the process to determine the goals. They will know something about why a goal was chosen. A well-articulated and debated goal hierarchy communicates criteria to team members for subsequent decisions. It permits decentralization of choices. Informed team members are less likely to escalate a conflict, and more likely to resolve it themselves.

The New Program Team

The new program team developed its program plan. They noted the changes from traditional practice and regarded them as challenges that would require special efforts. Most of the changes were substantial increases in the amount of lateral coordination. Their next task was to design the types and amounts of lateral organization. The next sections describe the design of the formal group structure. This is followed by a discussion of the concurrent design product development process, which was implemented to reduce development time from 24 to 18 months.

Formal Group Structure

The design of the formal groups followed from the lateral coordination requirements that were implied by the mission statement. The team first identified where increased coordination was required and then crafted a structure of teams. This structure is multidimensional and hierarchical.

Coordination Requirements

There were four areas where lateral coordination requirements were salient. Each was a derivative of the lowest-cost objective.

1. **Marketing Integration.** One of the keys to attaining lowest cost was volume. Volume would achieve discounts on pur-

chased components. As purchased materials were 80 percent of the cost of goods sold, volume was critical.

One source of increased volume was greater sales of the product. Currently, Hewlett-Packard sold only to customers who purchased Hewlett-Packard systems. Therefore, the product needed to be designed to sell into the three larger markets, in addition to the H-P market. These other three markets were for IBM systems customers, DEC customers, and the general standard market (ASCII).

These were new markets for the Terminals Division. The design engineers did not know the market requirements for these products. Therefore, the marketing function needed to research the markets and work with product design engineers to formulate new product specifications. This tighter integration with marketing was new. It would require marketing to be stronger and to become involved in the design process earlier.

2. Global Coordination. The required sales volume also meant that the products had to be sold outside the United States; they had to be global products. Therefore, global product requirements had to be determined. The products would also have to be produced in Europe by the Grenoble Division. Therefore, the design effort had to be coordinated with international marketing and the Grenoble Division. These interfaces had been used before, but the cost and speed requirements meant that more coordination would be needed this time.

3. Purchasing Coordination. The real volume necessary was purchasing volume from suppliers. This volume could be increased through increased sales volume by sharing components with other products in the division and by focusing volume on just a few suppliers.

The team had to coordinate the design of components—like cathode ray tubes (CRTs), printed circuit boards (PCBs), and keyboards—with other design groups for the division's other products. Then the division had to reduce and select the number of suppliers that it uses. It would have to negotiate new cost and quality supply agreements with these chosen suppliers. This effort must coordinate design, quality, and purchasing people for different components on different products.

4. Design Coordination. The design had to be guided by low-cost considerations, and it had to minimize the number of parts and components. In addition, it had to be easily manufactured and repaired. Product quality and reliability had to be designed into the product from the beginning. The implication was that manufacturing engineers, quality engineers, and purchasing negotiators had to join the marketers and design engineers in early integration into the design process.

Tight coordination and communication among all functions was needed to achieve the lowest-cost, highest-quality product design. Even more coordination was needed to produce the design and manufacture in 18 months. A 25 percent time compression would require intense coordination.

For all these reasons, the new mission for the division required new types—and increased amounts of—lateral organization. A new structure of cross-functional, cross-divisional teams was needed.

Team Structure

The new program team designed a new, sophisticated team structure in order to meet the new coordination requirements. The structure is multidimensional, hierarchical, and interlinked.

The new program team consisted of three subteams. There was one for hardware product design, one for software development, and one for the localization of hardware and software to meet various local requirements in different countries. The total structure is shown in Fig. 7.3.

The hardware team was further subdivided into manufacturing teams around several assembly processes. There was also a team for each major component that was to be purchased and negotiated. And, finally, a negotiating team was created to negotiate the contracts for components that were to be designed and shared across the division.

The linkages among the teams are critical. The new program team is the integrating forum for most issues. This team is a cross-functional group led by the new program manager and two architects. An architect is usually a generalist who knows a good deal about hardware, software, and systems integration. On this program, there are two because the chief architect had

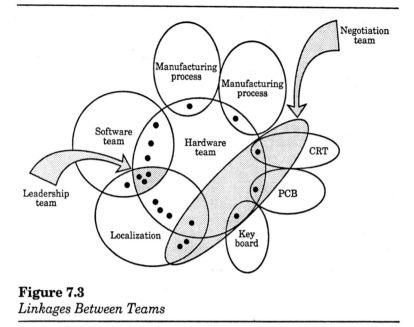

Figure 7.3
Linkages Between Teams

no international experience. A second, internationally experienced architect was added to form a leadership triumvirate with the program manager.

There are several liaison engineers who serve as linkages between hardware and software design. These people are generalists who are future architects. (The architects are future program managers.) The liaison engineers will convene whatever group is necessary to problem solve around hardware/software interfaces.

The linkage between the localization team and the hardware and software design teams was managed with joint staffing; that is, some engineers were members of both teams. The design teams had members from the major international divisions. These members were to suggest product requirements to the design team. The intention was to make the product design easily modifiable from the beginning. The costs of localization are greatly reduced if subsequent modifications are anticipated and can be done with software. Conflicts about designs are escalated to the leadership group of the program manager and the architects.

The hardware team is the most complicated, because of its many interfaces. These interfaces are necessary to get the early input to design truly lowest-cost products. The most complex interface was managed with teams for major components that were shared with other division products. If other division product teams were interested in lowest-cost, the coordination problem was easier. The division mission and cross-functional goals (and the prior discussions) were foundations for the design decisions.

The hardware design team spent several weeks touring the Far East, studying low-cost components, their vendors, and their capabilities. Only then did the initial design begin. Members of the design team who visited the Far East took the leader roles of the component teams. These teams consisted of engineers from design, quality, purchasing, and manufacturing and financial analysts. The design engineers came from all product lines. A steering committee was created for fast resolution of disagreements in commonality. Total cost was the major criterion, but occasionally superior performance would lead to competitive advantage for a product with a customized component. The steering committee was chaired by the head of R&D and staffed with the purchasing managers for Terminals and Grenoble, as well as the product architects.

A negotiating team then revisited the suppliers to negotiate product and price agreements. They brought with them the preliminary design specifications. The team consisted of the leaders of the component teams, designers, purchasing people from both divisions, and financial analysts. They would visit the vendor during the day and make design modifications at night, if needed. At completion, they achieved 90 percent commonality across product lines at Terminals and Grenoble. The commonality gave them the volume to achieve significant cost reductions. Eventually the vendors became qualified, which allowed in-house inspection to be eliminated.

The other interface for the hardware design team was with manufacturing process teams. These teams consisted of product design engineers, manufacturing process design engineers, quality engineers, and manufacturing managers and blue-collar workers. A team of experienced assemblers was created and placed in the process teams.

In this manner, multidimensional groups were formed. Teams were created for hardware, software, localization, purchased components, and manufacturing processes. These teams were placed in a hierarchy of the new program team: first, its leadership team; then the hardware, software, and localization; and, finally, component and manufacturing teams, which are subparts of the hardware team. The various levels and dimensions were linked by liaison roles, joint staffing, and subteam leaders as members of next-level teams. These teams represented the increased amounts and types of lateral coordination required by the new mission.

Concurrent Design

The new program effort was characterized by early entry into the design process of the other functions and divisions involved in the product design and manufacture. Usually, product design with one or a few product marketing people began the design. Other functions would enter when their turn came around. On the new program, the design engineers were joined by designers (mostly engineers) from all of the other functions. In addition, the product development time was to be compressed by 25 percent. The new program represented a substantial increase in lateral coordination across functions and divisions.

The design process started by being market-driven; that is, global customer requirements, comparisons with competitive offerings, and the search for competitive advantage drove the design process. The requirements were determined from customer surveys, focus groups, discussions with international marketing people, and the involvement of marketing people from the Grenoble Division. The engineers simultaneously disassembled and examined, piece by piece, the nine most competitive products. The result was a determination of what was important to the customer, how the competitive products met those requirements, and the choice of product-design targets for the new program team. The new role taken by marketing was a change from their previous nonleader role.

The next change was designing for low cost and for manufacturability. The concurrent design process, which was now being implemented, involved bringing in manufacturing engineers early in the process and making them partners to the design. Implementation of concurrent design (also called simultaneous engineering) was easier said than done. Design engineers do not always welcome others into their creative process. The transition to concurrent design was supported by four factors that were put into place at the Terminals Division. The first was the up-front debate and consensus on the mission. The implications of the mission were known and discussed in advance. Second, the advanced knowledge of the mission permitted selection and self-selection of engineers. Some engineers opted out and moved to other product lines and other divisions in H-P. Those engineers whose skills and interests matched the mission were selected for the new program.

The third factor was an H-P-wide change to upgrade manufacturing engineers. Typically, product design engineers at H-P who did not keep up technically migrated to manufacturing and quality engineering. They became second-class citizens. However, H-P recognized the need for low-cost hardware manufacturing skills. They began to upgrade manufacturing engineers. New hires were recruited from college, and high-talent transfers were orchestrated. Now manufacturing engineers could become true partners with design engineers.

Finally, division management issued challenges to the engineers: Can you really minimize the number of parts? How low a cost can you achieve? Several application-specific semiconductor designs were also needed. Could the engineers minimize the number of semiconductor chips? Management tried to make lowest-cost design as challenging as high-performance design. With the engineers that were selected, management was successful. The number of parts was reduced by 30 percent, the number of vendors by 40 percent. The overall cost of raw materials and components was reduced by 50 percent, while the number of engineering changes was also reduced by 50 percent. The lateral organization had achieved the lateral coordination.

Life Cycle Coordination

The cross-functional coordination that was achieved by concurrent design was to be extended across the entire life cycle of a product. Life cycle management arises due to compressed product life cycles in the marketplace. The team managing a product is to get the product into all the markets quickly at inception and phase it out at termination with a minimum of obsolescent inventory. The team is to manage a product start to finish.

One of the benefits of compressed development times and life cycles is the possibility of team continuity over the product's useful life. The program manager and the core program team were dedicated to the effort for at least three years. This continuity resulted in a high level of motivation for the team. Life-cycle responsibility gave the team a complete task; they had to live with their early decision. As a result, they set goals to make this the most profitable total program at H-P. The ownership of the start-to-finish responsibility has resulted in—and continues to offer—higher levels of team camaraderie and motivation.

The program team developed a life cycle responsibility chart. The chart is shown in Fig. 7.4. The chart lists the division's functions on one axis and the phases of the program on the other axis. In each cell of the chart is the function's responsibility during that phase of the program. The up-front discussion and negotiation of roles led to a collective understanding of roles and responsibilities. The chart was then discussed with all work groups involved in the program. Eventually, the chart was printed and pasted in all the work areas for all employees to see.

A new core team has been created for the next-generation product. The team leader and some team members are gradu-

	Investigation	Design	Transition	Manufacturing	Discontinuance
Marketing	Responsibilities ———————————————————▶				
R&D					
Manufacturing					
Quality					
Support					
Finance					

Review

Figure 7.4
Life Cycle Responsibility Chart

ates of the new program team. They too are employing life-cycle management. The new team has already set cost and quality targets to improve on those of the new program. The most aggressive objective is to reduce the product development time to 12 months.

Global Coordination

The new program was not only to design a lowest-cost product in 18 months, but also to design a global product; that is, the product was to be introduced simultaneously in all world markets, with a minimum of local redesign. The new program team had representatives from the Grenoble Division and communicated with international marketing representing the Far East. Other representatives from Grenoble joined the negotiating team that chose the suppliers and the component teams. They traveled with the teams to the Far East and made trips to the Terminals Division for meetings. The two divisions exchanged two engineers in design and manufacturing. Two engineers from Grenoble, on two-year assignments, worked at the Terminals Division, and vice versa. But it was the daily communication via H-P's internal computer network, phone, and fax that kept the Grenoble participants as members of the program team. The liaison engineers were very helpful in interpreting the E-mail and faxes.

H-P also employs a version of the distributed organization to link the Terminals and Grenoble Divisions. The Terminals Division has worldwide design responsibility for terminals. These designs are manufactured at the Terminals Division for North America and at the Grenoble Division for Europe. The Grenoble Division has worldwide design responsibility for low-end personal computers. Their designs are manufactured at the Grenoble Division for the European market and at the Terminals Division for the North American market. Thus, the relationship between the divisions is reciprocal and balanced. Global products are designed in only one place. Costs of duplication are eliminated in the high-fixed-cost design process. But each division has a worldwide responsibility. Each division works for the other on their respective worldwide mission. As a result, the two divisions are in constant communication with each other.

The new program team successfully employed concurrent design features to design and manufacture its lowest-cost product and to compress the development time to 18 months. In addition to concurrent design practices, the team also employed the distributed organization to achieve a global product, and a life cycle management responsibility to give the team total start-to-finish control of the product. These practices were all successful and are being refined and used again on future products.

Summary

The Terminals Division story provides a good capstone for the book. The division's experience is instructive because it illustrates how an organization can build the lateral capability as it needs it. Management invested considerable time and effort up front. Starting with themselves, they invested in skill-building and team-building. Then they immediately employed these skills in crafting a new mission and strategy to transform the division. Again, they invested in a process to cascade the skill-building and team-building throughout the entire organization. They played key roles in teaching the skills to the organization.

Management further invested time and effort in the planning process, to align division goals and functional goals. The planning effort also built on and reinforced the skills learned earlier. Management employed a number of tools to communicate and achieve a unified sense of purpose. The mission-statement discussion, the single-sheet portrayal of objectives, and the life cycle responsibility charts communicate to all employees what their part is in this shared effort.

The new program team built on this foundation to employ a very sophisticated formal group design. A very costly and complex large-scale effort was needed to match the magnitude of this coordination task. The teams were multidimensional to integrate products across functions, products across geographies, and components across products. Teams were multilevel to provide a hierarchy to resolve disagreements rapidly and achieve global integration. The teams were all linked at key points. The large effort achieved the purpose for which it was created.

The success was achieved at a great cost of management time and effort. However, the costs are an investment and not an expense, as current accounting practice considers such efforts. The investments of management have created a considerable organizational capability. This capability is an asset—an intangible asset. With this intangible asset, the Terminals Division has a real competitive advantage.

8

Summary Thoughts

In this last chapter, the key ideas presented in the book are revisited. These points were discussed throughout the book but are featured here to underline their importance.

Competing with Your Organization

The first idea to be stressed is the use of organizational capability as a competitive tool. In today's global economy, one competes with every means possible. It turns out that organizational capabilities are a particularly useful means. They allow a company to execute difficult tasks, such as design, and introduce global products rapidly. They are hard to duplicate without repeating the same capability-building efforts. Therefore, capabilities are being recognized as sustainable sources of competitive advantage.

Heretofore, managers did not think of organization as a competitive tool. Organization was a necessary evil—something to be circumvented, or something that headquarters was always changing. Managers focused on "good people." These good people are still needed, but they have to be grown and developed. As they are developed, an organization is also developed. The organization then facilitates the actions of these people. Ultimately the winners are those who get the most from their talent. Getting the most requires organization and organizational capabilities.

Lateral Organization as Flexible Organization

The second major point of the book is that an organizational capability that provides an advantage is the lateral organization. The advantage is that lateral organization provides the flexibility needed in today's ever-changing business environment. The flexibility is achieved in at least three ways:

First, the lateral organizational capability generates speed. Peer-to-peer collaboration is often better and faster than using the hierarchy. It focuses on pleasing the customer, not the boss.

Second, lateral organization is a multidimensional organization. It allows a focus on whatever dimension or issue is currently salient. The company can be responsive to multiple constituencies without having to reorganize to do it. The lateral capability allows the organization to flex and deal with an unforeseen issue. The lateral organization is an organization that is flexible and adaptable and suited for an uncertain and changing world.

Third, the lateral organization promotes learning and change. An organization structure simultaneously promotes execution of a given strategy and constrains the formulation of new strategies. An organization designed around today's strategy creates a constituency with a vested interest in the status quo. This constituency can prevent or slow a response to a changing world and can become a competitive disadvantage. A lateral organization can create multiple dimensions and multiple constituencies. As a result, there is always a voice for change.

These voices for continuity and change should be channeled into the planning process. The planning process is then less of a process to create a plan and more a vehicle to promote learning. Thus the successful implementation of lateral organizations creates a faster-learning, more rapidly changing organization. There is always a constituency for change.

Different Types of Lateral Organization

The use of teams runs the risk of becoming a panacea. Today's press describes teams as an almost universal solution to management's ills. In this book, a key point was that there are different types and amounts of lateral organization. Simple teams were one of several designs to execute strategies.

The point stressed in this book was to match the types and amounts of lateral organization with the lateral coordination requirements of the strategies. Different strategies will require different types and amounts of lateral organization. Implicit is the notion that lateral organization carries costs and benefits. It is possible to have too much or too little lateral organization. The lesson should be to start with strategy and prescribe only the types and amounts of lateral organization that are required for execution.

Management's Role

Management's role was highlighted throughout the book. In addition to articulating strategy, two roles were specific to the lateral organization. The first role was to match the types and amounts of lateral organization to the strategy-implementation requirements. This book has tried to articulate how to make this match. The second role is to build the lateral organizational capability so that the types and amounts of lateral organization can be drawn upon when needed. The building of this capability requires substantial investment in people development and information technology. Building organizational capability is therefore like building any technical or distribution capability. It is built through sustained investment, and linked to strategy in order to gain an advantage and create value for customers.

Summary

In the digital world of tomorrow, where competitive advantage is man-made, companies will compete by using their organization. In order to compete effectively, companies will require some types of lateral organizational capability. This capability will need to be employed in various amounts at different times. A management that has built the capability and is skilled at matching it to strategies will gain a competitive advantage.

Bibliography

Allen, Thomas. 1977. *(Title unknown at this moment)*. Cambridge, MA: MIT Press.

Bartlett, C. A. 1983. "MNC's: Get off the Reorganization Merry-Go-Round." *Harvard Business Review,* (March–April): 138–146.

Bartlett, C. A., and Sumantra Goshal. 1989. *Managing Across Borders.* Boston: Harvard Business School Press.

Cohen, S. G. 1993. "Teams and Teamwork: Future Directions." In Galbraith and Lawler. *The Future of Organizations.* San Francisco: Jossey-Bass.

Dyer, W. G. 1988. *Team Building: Issues and Alternatives.* Reading, MA: Addison-Wesley.

Eccles, R. G., and D. B. Crane. 1988. *Doing Deals.* Boston: Harvard Business School Press.

Edstrom, A. and J. R. Galbraith. 1977. "Transfer of Managers as a Coordination and Control Strategy in Multi-National Corporations." *Administrative Science Quarterly,* 22: 248–263.

Evans, P., A. Laurent, and Y. Doz (eds.) 1989. *Human Resource Management in International Firms: Change, Globalization, Innovation.* London: MacMillan

Fayol, H. 1925. *Industrial and General Administration.* Translation 1949. London: Pitman & Sons.

Galbraith, J. R. 1973. *Designing Complex Organizations.* Reading, MA: Addison-Wesley.

Galbraith, J. R. 1977. *Organization Design.* Reading, MA: Addison-Wesley.

Galbraith, J. R. 1982. "The Stages of Growth." *Journal of Business Strategy* (Summer): 70–79.

Galbraith, J. R. "Organization Design." In J. Lorsch (ed.) 1987. *Handbook of Organization Behavior.* Englewood Cliffs, NJ: Prentice-Hall.

Galbraith, J. R. 1993. "The Value Adding Corporation." In Galbraith and Lawler. *The Future of Organizations.* San Francisco: Jossey-Bass.

Galbraith, J. R., and R. Kazanjian. 1986. *Strategy Implementation.* St. Paul, MN: West Publishing.

Goggins, W. 1974. "How the Multi-Dimensional Structure Works at Dow Corning." *Harvard Business Review* 52: 54–65.

Grant, R. M. 1991. "The Resource-Based Theory of Competitive Advantage." *California Management Review* 33: 114–135.

Grant, R. M., A. Jamine, and J. Thomas. 1988. "Diversity, Diversification and Profitability Among British Manufacturing Companies 1972–1984." *Academy of Managment Journal* 31, No. 4: 771–801.

Hamel, G., and C. K. Prahalad. 1989. "Strategic Intent." *Harvard Business Review* 89 (3): 63–76.

Hammer, M. 1990. "Re-Engineering Work: Don't Automate, Obliterate." *Harvard Business Review* (July–August): 104–112.

Heygate, R., and G. Brebach. 1991. "Memo to a CEO: Corporate Re-Engineering." *McKinsey Quarterly* 2: 44–55.

Itami, H. 1987. *Mobilizing Invisible Assets.* Cambridge, MA: Harvard University Press.

Johansen, R. 1988. *Groupware.* New York: Free Press.

Kaplan, R. B., and C. Murdock. 1991. "Core Process Redesign." *McKinsey Quarterly* 2: 27–43.

Kirkpatrick, D. 1992. "Payoff from PCs." *Fortune* (March 23): 93–102.

Lawler, E. E. 1988. "Substitute for Hierarchy." *Organization Dynamics* 17 (1): 4–15.

Lawler, E. E. 1990. *Strategic Pay: Aligning Organizational Strategies and Pay Systems.* San Francisco: Jossey-Bass.

Lawler, E. E. 1992. *The Ultimate Advantage.* San Francisco: Jossey-Bass.

Lawler, E. E., and J. R. Galbraith. 1993. "The New Staff." In Galbraith and Lawler. *The Future of Organizations.* San Francisco: Jossey-Bass.

Lawrence, P., and J. Lorsch. 1967. *Organization and Environment.* Homewood, IL: Irwin.

Mytelka, L. K. 1991. *Strategic Partnerships and the World Economy.* Madison, NJ: Farleigh Dickinson Press.

Ostroff, F., and D. Smith. 1992. "The Horizontal Organization." *McKinsey Quarterly* (1): 148–167.

Peters, T. 1992. *Liberation Management.* New York: Knopf.

Porter, M. 1985. *Competitive Advantage.* New York: Free Press.

Porter, M. 1986. *Competition in Global Industries.* Boston: Harvard Business School Press.

Prahalad, C. K., and Y. Doz. 1987. *Multi-National Mission.* New York: Free Press.

Prahalad, C. K., and G. Hamel. 1990. "The Core Competence of the Corporation. *Harvard Business Review* (May–June): 79–91.

Pucik, V., N. Tichey, and C. Barnett. 1992. *Globalizing Management.* New York: Wiley.

Savage, C. 1992. *The Fifth Dimension.* Maynard, MA: Digital Press.

Simon, Herbert. 1960. *The New Science of Management Decision.* Englewood Cliffs, NJ: Prentice-Hall.

Smith, D., and J. Katzenbach. 1992. *The Wisdom of Teams.* Boston: Harvard Business School Press.

Stalk, G., and T. Hout. 1990. *Competing Against Time.* New York: Free Press.

Stalk, G., P. Evans, and L. Schulman. 1992. "Competing on Capabilities: The New Rules of Corporate Strategy." *Harvard Business Review* (March–Apr'l): 57–69.

Taylor, W. 1991. "The Logic of Global Business." *Harvard Business Review* (March–April): 91–105.

Thurow, L. 1992. *Head to Head.* New York: Morrow.

Tushman, M., and D. Nadler. 1988. *Strategic Organization Design.* Glenview, IL: Scott Foresman.

Wernerfelt, B. 1984. "A Resource-Based View of the Firm." *Management Journal* (5): 171–180.

Womack, J. P., D. T. Jones, and D. Roos. 1990. *The Machine That Changed the World.* New York: Maxwell MacMillan International.